Negro

in the

United States

Harold Van Buren Voorhis

Negro Masonry in the United States
By: Harold Van Buren Voorhis

Printed: November, 2003

Published and Distributed by:
LUSHENA BOOKS, INC.
607 Country Club Drive, Unit E
Bensenville, IL 60106

ISBN: 1-1930097-67-0

Printed in the United States of America

Original Charter of African Lodge, No. 459, granted by the Grand Lodge of England, September 29, 1784

INTRODUCTION

Grand Masters come and Grand Masters go to join the great majority in the Grand East as Past Grand Masters, but the research worker in the musty library corner, where are the forgotten old records, goes patiently on year after year without end and all too often without even decent recognition of his services to the Craft.

Worshipful Brother Harold V. B. Voorhis has many times put the Fraternity heavily in his debt. Comes he now with this most readable volume which in addition to being fascinating romance in a curious bypath across little known Masonic fields, clears up many a misconception which lack of documented literature has permitted to grow in the minds of the reading Masonic public.

The story of Alpha Lodge of New Jersey has been told before, but has so often been distorted in the Masonic (and secular!) press, that this contribution to its history and to the final (it is devoutly hoped!) settlement of the "mystery" which some prejudiced minds have made of its quite orderly and commonplace beginnings, is surely a contribution of note to American Masonic history.

This book is the result of nearly a quarter of a century of research. Research, too, of a particularly difficult character. Inasmuch as the records kept by recognized Freemasonry are often sketchy, frequently scanty and occasionally represented only by a blank, it is not a matter of wonder that Prince Hall Masonry should be difficult to trace with accuracy and completeness. This historian, whose patience is only equalled by his "nose for news" and his bulldog ability to stick to a trail long after less tenacious workers would have given up, has in this volume told the whole story of Negroes and Freemasonry with such authority, and in such a manner, that it will unquestionably become a standard work of reference on its subject. It takes the place of long out of print histories—in themselves largely inaccurate—and brings to library shelves a volume which is authentic, comprehensive, and clear.

v

INTRODUCTION

Perhaps nothing in the work is more appealing than the manner of presentation, which has been so finely balanced between love of historical accuracy on one hand, and devotion to recognized Freemasonry on the other, that it will be read with equal pleasure by both white and colored men. The author has written with neither prejudice nor passion, and if some of his conclusions are slightly unpalatable to some historians, justice demands that even they recognize that the facts, not the method of presentation, make them so.

The Masonic world is the richer for these labors of so ardent and skilled a worker in the quarries.

CARL H. CLAUDY

Washington, D. C.
November 22, 1939

CONTENTS

PART I — "UNRECOGNIZED" NEGRO MASONRY

PART II — RECOGNIZED NEGRO FREEMASONRY

APPENDIX

CONTENTS

ILLUSTRATIONS

PREFACE

No subject connected with Freemasonry is more complex, more open to varied discussion and less understood, although there is an abundance of historical source material available, than Negro Masonry. In referring to this subject, Samuel Evans, Past Master of Gate of the Temple Lodge in Massachusetts, once said, "No question is more affected by prejudice. Blood is thicker than creed. Difference of religious faith among Masons would not create one-tenth part of the commotion, as the raising of this question of race does. On this question of affiliation with races of all colors, or of one particular color, the men of the Past, the men of the Present, and the men of the Future have distinct ideas and feeling."

The "story" hereinafter presented is in no wise an historical treatise on the subject. It is a recording of the important events in the evolution of a phase of Masonry and primarily written to be read by the Master Mason. It is intended to give the reader a rather detailed outline of everything of importance having a bearing on the history of the Craft among the Negro brethren. It is the result of years of reading and particular research upon the subject.

There will undoubtedly be some who will not agree with the conclusions expressed on this or that occurrence, but every effort has been made to make a faithful interpretation when the elements of discussion may appear to place the conclusion in the balance. Resort to the opinions of the best informed Masons, of both races, has frequently been made so that conclusions, when expressed, may be the consensus of views held on a given point.

It must be borne in mind, by readers of both races, that the author is neither an apologist for the one nor the champion of condemnation for the other. The mission of this book is to present facts—as historically accurate as documentation can make them.

Short historical items on Negro Freemasonry in Masonic magazines, Proceedings and other literature of the Craft appear from the very beginning of the nineteenth century. The earliest printed work with a title indicating it to be exclusively devoted to Negro Freemasonry is a thirty-two page pamphlet published in Pittsburgh, Pennsylvania, in 1853. It is titled "The Origin and Objects of Ancient Freemasonry; Its Introduction into the United States and the Legitimacy Among Colored Men. A Treatise Delivered before St. Cyprian Lodge, No. 13, June 24th, A.D. 1853—A.L. 5853." The author, Martin R. Delaney, M.D., was born at Charlestown, Virginia, on May 6, 1812 and died at Pittsburgh, Pennsylvania, on January 24, 1885. He was the first Negro to receive a commission in the Medical Corps of the Union Army in the Civil War, having been appointed a Major in the 104th Regiment of South Carolina by President Abraham Lincoln, serving on the staff of General Daniel E. Sickles. Later he served on the staff of Governor Scott of South Carolina with the rank of Lieutenant-Colonel. As a historical work, the pamphlet is without value, being mostly devoted to a discussion on the state of man and of the subject of slavery in its relation to Freemasonry.

Only three books have been published, the contents of which are devoted entirely to Negro Freemasonry—all three being out of print and very difficult to secure in the used book market.

The first is "Negro Masonry, Being a Critical Examination of Objections to the Legitimacy of the Masonry Existing Among the Negroes of America" by William H. Upton, Past Grand Master of the Grand Lodge of Washington (white), published by the M.˙.W.˙. Prince Hall Grand Lodge of Massachusetts in 1902. It is an 8vo. book of 264 pages. This work first appeared as a report to the Grand Lodge of the State of Washington in 1899 and then in the form of an 8vo., 137 page book, the same year, in Seattle, Washington. It had a slightly different title, the first part being "Light on a Dark Subject" instead of "Negro Masonry." The 1902 edition is nearly twice the size of the original. The first two issues are rarely seen. The author was a qualified Masonic historian and the work is exceptionally well documented and, in the main, dependable. It is a defence of Negro Freemasonry rather than a history.

x

The second is an "Official History of Freemasonry Among the Colored People of North America," by William H. Grimshaw, Past Deputy Grand Master of the Grand Lodge of the District of Columbia (Prince Hall). It is a 12mo. book of 393 pages, copyrighted in 1903 and published in New York, N.Y. It is a sort of "historical treatise" but the data are frequently untrustworthy—that outside of symbolic Masonry being practically useless, from an historical point of view. Nevertheless it can be considered the only extensive history in print of Prince Hall or Negro Freemasonry and is usually the only book to be found in our Masonic libraries on the subject.

The third is "Prince Hall and His Followers," by George W. Crawford, 33°, present Lt. Sov. Grand Commander of United Supreme Council, A. A. S. R., Northern Jurisdiction (Prince Hall Affiliation). It is an 8vo. book of 96 pages published in New York in 1914. It is a monograph on the legitimacy of Negro Masonry, and like the Upton book, it cannot be classed as a history.

Numerous pamphlets, some rather extensive, have appeared on different phases of the subject. Nearly all are scarce and frequently unavailable even in our larger Masonic libraries.

That portion of this work which constitutes the history of Alpha Lodge, No. 116, of Newark, New Jersey, is a complete revision of the first printed history of the lodge ever to appear. Written by the author it is to be found in the Transactions of the North Carolina Lodge of Research, No. 666, A. F. & A. M., "Nocalore," Volume II, Part 3, 1932.

Two unpublished manuscripts, historical treatises, are ready for publication, but like many historical works on Freemasonry, printing is being held up awaiting the return of a reading Masonic public of sufficient size to warrant a financial outlay to cover cost of production. One is "The Prince Hall Sodality," by W.˙.Brother Harry E. Davis, 33°, of Cleveland, Ohio, Special Deputy for Foreign Relations, Grand Lodge of Ohio (Prince Hall). The other is "The History of Freemasonry Among the American Negroes," by R.˙.W.˙. Brother Harry A. Williamson, 32°, of New York, N. Y., Past Deputy Grand Master, Grand Lodge of New York (Prince Hall).

I am particularly indebted to both of these brethren for their aid in making rare publications and source manuscript material available to me, as well as their willing assistance in the preparation of this work. They are both exceptionally qualified historians and have labored long and faithfully among the archives of the Craft.

In concluding—I suggest that the following pages be read with an open, unprejudiced and unbiased mind. The best way to do that, it seems to me, is for the reader to consider himself of the opposite race during the perusal of these pages. If this is done, a fairly correct picture of Negro Freemasonry as a whole will surely be obtained. I even suggest re-reading once or twice, because it is a difficult subject "beset with many dangers," but I am confident that it will be found to be interesting. I have found that thousands of our brethren have become absorbed in the story as I have told it orally in more than a hundred Masonic bodies.

HAROLD VAN BUREN VOORHIS, P.M.

Red Bank, New Jersey
July 4, 1939

NEGRO MASONRY
IN THE UNITED STATES

FOREWORD TO PART ONE

This book has been written in two parts because the subject of Negro Freemasonry really has two distinct stories. Neither dovetails into the other or has to do with each other. The first part deals with Negro Freemasonry which is not "recognized" by that Freemasonry in the United States which designates itself "regular."

The subject is one about which the white Freemason is not even vaguely familiar. In a general way the Negro Freemason knows something of his history, just as the white Freemason knows the general facts connected with his. But, because this subject is replete with comparisons between "recognized" and "unrecognized" Freemasonry, the task of presenting the picture clearly is not simple.

The first difficulty is to determine what to include and what to leave out without affecting the true picture. To this is added the necessity of going into jurisprudence angles which are not common knowledge on the part of the Master Mason. Aside and beyond these things, there is the element of difference of opinion, which so largely enters into this story. The whole idea of this book, as mentioned in the Preface, is to give the facts in such a manner that they may be easily understood and profitably read. But it becomes necessary in certain places to record some rather intricate and, without doubt, some confusing things—from the laymen's point of view. It is regrettable that recourse to these intricate and confusing points must be had, but there seems no other way to give a full picture of the situation. If a review of the rise of Negro Freemasonry were given without referring to or comparing it with "recognized" Freemasonry, the final picture would be but a bare sketch without the background or shading to complete it.

Freemasonry is divided into two groups—Recognized and Unrecognized Freemasonry. Under the first grouping are those bodies which "recognize" each other, Masonically, and often described as "Regular" bodies. To this group belong the State Grand Lodges of white Freemasons in the United States. The second group is composed of "unrecognized and irregular or clandestine" bodies—two distinct classes. It has become a habit, by usage, to consider the terms "irregular" and "clandestine" as synonymous—and often Masonic legislation has been written on this basis.

Because the fact has been lost sight of that an "unrecognized" Masonic body may be perfectly "regular," and not be "recognized" (as were all which are now in the "recognized" group—before recognition), the "unrecognized," though "regular" part of the second group of Freemasons, has come to be considered in the same category as those that are irregular or clandestine.

A clandestine Masonic body is one that has been set up since organized Grand Lodge Freemasonry was formed, without any authority of any kind, by individuals grouping themselves into such a body. They may or may not have been Freemasons previously.

An irregular Masonic body is one whose "working" was once recognized, but because of some Masonic impropriety, is no longer recognized, no matter how regular it once was.

Both classes may, under certain conditions, become recognized by "healing," changing or removing their offending reasons for non-recognition, etc., etc.

There remains a much larger group—those whose Masonic regularity is quite normal, and yet who have not been "recognized." In this group are the Negro brethren.

To understand what follows, it is necessary to bear this difference of classification in mind and to remember that regularity and recognition are not the same thing.

It becomes necessary, also, to caution the reader that in those places where a "tearing apart" of statements of "historians" of the last century is resorted to, it is not in any way saying, in effect, that "recognized" Freemasonry is not within its province when it continues its non-recognition of Negro Masonry. It is the illogical and frequently unfair methods used by some of our white brethren in trying to "explain" the situation, which are exposed. Too often writers have failed to look at both sides of the matter and have frequently extracted material to prove this or that point which, if

4

completely used, would nullify the very objective of their attack. The nearest approach to reason for such tactics seems to be that in these instances prejudice is the blinding force—for these same writers on other subjects are peers in their field. This gives undue credulousness to their opinions on Negro Freemasonry and, by the unsuspecting, their statements are absorbed *in toto*.

Over a period of many years I have read hundreds of discussions and opinions in Grand Lodge proceedings on this subject—among which are some of the most vitriolic attacks on Negroes and Negro Freemasonry. Yet, during the times when these attacks were in especially full bloom, as well as during periods of quiescence, there is only the evidence of our Negro brethren facing the issue very calmly as gentlemen. As I now look back upon the picture I cannot but feel that the white brethren have not added to their stature by their actions. The mountains builded out of mole-hills have not withstood the elements of careful scrutiny and are being leveled by the plumb of reason and the square of honest judgment. Had fewer oral stones been thrown many more glass houses might now be standing.

I give, therefore, out of the unbelievable mass of material available, the following resumé of that which I believe necessary for a fairly full picture of the history of Negro Freemasonry in the United States.

PART I

"UNRECOGNIZED" NEGRO FREEMASONRY

CHAPTER 1

PRINCE HALL

*N*EGRO Freemasonry in the United States can trace its origin to the first Negro who was made a Freemason in the "New World." This important figure, Prince Hall, was born in Bridgetown, Barbadoes, British West Indies, on September 12, 1748, according to Grimshaw. Worshipful Bro. Davis (Grand Lodge of Ohio, Prince Hall) does not accept this date, however. He has copies of two death notices of Hall from the BOSTON GAZETTE and INDEPENDENT CHRONICLE, dated Monday, December 7, 1807, which give his age as seventy-two years. This would make his birth year 1735. Also, these notices state Hall's death as occurring on Friday morning, which would make the date December 4th instead of the 7th as recorded by Grimshaw and others, which is obviously incorrect. Prince Hall was the son of Thomas Prince Hall, an Englishman, then a leather merchant, whose wife was a free Negro woman of French descent.

Hall, whose "given" name "Prince" was in no way a title, was apprenticed by his father to the leather trade at the age of twelve years. A few years at the task convinced him that future prospects, locally, were very meager. He therefore determined to come to the American mainland Colonies and obtained a "working passage" aboard a ship bound for Boston, where he arrived in March, 1765. Here he soon found employment and by economical living, in the space of eight years, saved enough to become a freeholder and voter. He also enriched his mind by lessons during the evening hours. In 1774 we find him among the converts of Richard Bondman and Joseph Gilmore, missionaries of the Methodist Church. He began a study of the Bible, which culminated in his admission to the Christian Ministry. In his capacity of Clergyman in Cambridge, Massachusetts, he soon became a spiritual and social leader of the colored people in and about the city.

In 1775, on behalf of the colored freemen of Boston, he presented a petition to John Hancock and Joseph Warren, of the Committee of Safety of the Colonies, asking for permission to join the Army. The petition was denied but at the same time referred to Congress (June 6, 1775), where it died "on the table." It was then referred to General Washington, who granted it to the extent of continuing in service free Negroes with the Army at Cambridge. By this and subsequent acts, Hall soon gave evidence of his Colonial sympathies so that in February, 1776, he joined the American Army. After his military service he returned to Boston in 1782 and married Phoebe Baker, a resident of that city. This was not Hall's first venture into matrimony, however. In Copp's Hill Burying Ground, Boston, there is a stone on which is found, "Sarah Richery, wife of Prince Hall, died February 26th, 1769, aged 24 years." On the back of the stone is the record of the burial of Hall himself. The whereabouts of the remains of Phoebe Baker are not known. It is known, however, that she was still alive in 1813.

On January 13, 1777, Hall filed a memorial addressed "To the Honorable Council and House of Representatives for the State of Massachusetts Bay, in General Court Assembled," urging emancipation.

On October 17, 1787 he again petitioned the Legislature to provide educational facilities for colored children. In his "Charge Delivered to the Brethren of the African Lodge on the 25th of June, 1792," (see illustration), he said, "let us lay by our recreation, and superfluities, so that we may have that to educate our rising generation, which was spent in these follies. Make you this beginning, and who knows but God may raise up some friend or body of friends as he did in Philadelphia, to open a School for the blacks here, as that friendly city has done there." On October 4, 1796, the Selectmen of the Town of Boston were sent a Memorial on this school matter, and before the end of the year such a school was established.

On February 27, 1788, after the kidnapping of three Colored free-men, one a Masonic brother of Hall and a member of his Lodge, he addressed a petition to the "Senate and House of Representatives of the Commonwealth of Massachusetts," protesting against the outrage. It was signed by Hall and twenty-two members of his Lodge. The result was freedom and a return of the kidnapped men. (The white Freemasons joined Hall in this effort.)

On November 26, 1786, when Shay's Rebellion broke out, Hall wrote Governor Bowdoin offering the services of the entire member-ship of his Lodge. A part of the letter, shown because of its Masonic flavor, was as follows:

"We, by the Providence of God, are members of a fraternity that not only enjoins upon us to be peaceable subjects to the civil powers where we reside, but it also forbids our having concern in any plot or conspiracies against the state where we dwell," etc.

Aside from his connection with the advent of Negro Freemasonry in the United States, we are not particularly concerned with the facts of his life. Suffice it, therefore, to record that early in November, 1807 he was stricken with pneumonia and, after an illness of a month, passed away on December 4th. His remains were deposited in Copp's Hill Burying Ground, Boston, following impressive cere-monies attended by a large number of Boston citizens of both races. A monument was unveiled at his grave on June 25, 1895 with Past Grand Master, John J. Smith, the only surviving member of African Lodge, present. (Initiated April 18, 1846.)

CHAPTER 2

PRINCE HALL MADE A FREEMASON

*I*N 1899 Prince Hall's "Letter Book" was found. It contained a record of his correspondence and sermons from 1782 to 1806. At the same time a few of the early minutes, memoranda and pertinent material bearing on the early activities of Negro Masonry in Boston and Philadelphia were also found. The entire collection of material has never been published but is among the archives of the Prince Hall Grand Lodge of Massachusetts in the safe deposit vault of a Boston trust company, where the original Charter of African Lodge, No. 459, also rests.

From the records we find that on March 6, 1775, Prince Hall and the colored men listed later in this Chapter, were initiated in a Lodge of Freemasons at Castle William, Boston Harbor (now Fort Independence) by the Master of Lodge No. 441 (a military lodge on the Irish Registry), attached to the 38th Foot (Regiment) whose existence is verified by the Masonic historian Robert Freke Gould. The Master of the Lodge, at the time of the initiation, was Sergeant J. B. Batt. The British War Department has verified that Sergeant Batt was in Major Andrew Bruce's Company of the 38th Foot and that his name appears on all its preserved Muster Rolls from the date of his enlistment in 1759 to his discharge at Staten Island in 1777. Batt's name appears on the old Register of the Grand Lodge of Ireland as a member of No. 441.

One version is that Hall went to the headquarters of General Gage, where the military lodge meetings were held, and was admitted to Freemasonry and raised the same evening, and that subsequently (March 6, 1775) the others were made Masons. No one has brought forth any evidence to substantiate this, but on the contrary, the records show that Hall and the fourteen others were all admitted on March 6th. Whether or not they received the three degrees or only one on that date is not known.

10

Prince Hall, first Negro made a Freemason in America

Names of Colored men received into Freemasonry on March 6, 1775

1. Prince Hall

2. Peter Best
3. Cuff Bufform
4. John Carter
5. Peter Freeman
6. Fortune Howard
7. Cyrus Jonbus
8. Prince Rees

9. Thomas Sanderson
10. Buesten Singer
11. Boston Smith
12. Cato Speain
13. Prince Taylar
14. Benjamin Tiber
15. Richard Tilley

The candidates paid fifteen guineas for Entering; seven for Passing; and three for Raising.

In commenting on the circumstances of the entrance of these first colored men in the Colonies into Freemasonry, M∴W∴William Sewall Gardner, Grand Master of the Grand Lodge of Massachusetts (white), in his address to Grand Lodge in 1870, said,

"I have no doubt that, on the 6th of March, 1775, the day after Warren delivered his celebrated oration in the Old South Church, where he was menaced by British troops, Prince Hall and thirteen others received the three degrees in a traveling lodge attached to one of the British regiments in the Army of General Gage, by whom Boston was then garrisoned."

M∴W∴Samuel W. Clark, "Grand Master of Colored Masons of the State of Ohio," in his "The Negro Mason in Equity," publicly delivered, and printed with the Proceedings of the Grand Lodge of Ohio (Negro) for 1885, in noting these remarks by M∴W∴Brother Gardner, said:

"The record of the initiation supplemented with the testimony of such an eminent Mason and scholar as William Sewall Gardner, who, probably, has given more study and research to this particular question than any other white Mason in America, should be sufficient to establish the falsity of the first objection, and to remove all doubts concerning our origin; and especially so when it is remembered that his historical researches are not for our benefit, but for our destruction. He is entitled to the

11

credit, however, of being a true historian, although his conclusions are not always philosophical."

At the Annual Communication of the Grand Lodge of Ohio (white) held on October 19, 1875, a Committee composed of Lucius V. Bierce, P.G.M.; Enoch T. Carson, P.M.; Ferdinand Wilmer, P.M.; Louis H. Pike, P.M.; and Charles A. Woodward, G.M. (1876) that was appointed to investigate the subject of Negro Masonry at the previous Annual Communication of Grand Lodge, presented their findings. The report, petition, memorials, and all data concerning the subject were assembled by order of the Grand Lodge by John D. Caldwell, the Grand Secretary. It covers fifty-six printed pages with Proceedings, and is entitled, "New Day —New Duty." It also appears in pamphlet form. Among the conclusions made by the Committee are these statements:

"Your Committee deem it sufficient to say that they are satisfied beyond all question that Colored Freemasonry had a legitimate beginning in this country as much so as any other Freemasonry; in fact it came from the same source.

"Your Committee have the most satisfactory and conclusive evidence that these Colored Freemasons practice the very same rites and ceremonies, and have substantially the same esoteric or secret modes of recognition as are practiced by ourselves and by the universal family of Freemasons throughout the world."

These statements were prepared before the discovery of the record of the entrance of Prince Hall and the fourteen others into the Craft came to light. It seems unnecessary to go further into the various discussions which have appeared during the last hundred years on this point. It appears to be established "beyond reasonable doubt" that Hall and his associates WERE made Freemasons in an Army Lodge which was regularly established—even though we may not have positively established the exact one.

There has been put forth the argument that the making of Prince Hall and the other colored men Freemasons in an Army lodge was an illegal act. Many rebuttals to this argument could be given to show that the practice was not illegal at all but rather a common proceeding, both in the American Colonies and elsewhere by Army lodges under English, Irish and Scottish Constitutions. (Not prohibited by England until 1815).

Assuming that the Lodge was under Irish Constitution, it would be working under a rule adopted in 1768 by the Grand Lodge of Ireland which prohibited an Army Lodge from making a civilian a Freemason when there was a "Town's Lodge" at the place of the quartering of the Regiment. There was not a single Irish Lodge in the whole of Massachusetts at the time—1775. To narrow down the interpretation of the rule to have it apply to any lodge—no matter what its registry might be—Castle William was two and a half miles from what was then the Town of Boston. As a matter of fact the place was not a part of any town, but, if the nearest one might be considered that town, then Dorchester would be the place and no lodge was established in Dorchester until many years after the date 1775.

It is often stated that on October 1, 1773, the Massachusetts Grand Lodge (Gardner) or the Provincial Grand Lodge of Massachusetts (Woodbury), voted that "the Lodge at Castle William nor no other Traveling Lodges, has any Right to Make Masons of any Citizen." Upon examination of the "vote" we find that it was on "The Petition of Richard Carpenter and Others" and not on the above quoted prohibition at all. Even though it were, it would have had no effect whatever, excepting the possibility of such made Masons visiting lodges under the jurisdiction legislating thereon.

All of the objections that have been made are in disregard of the rules and regulations of the period.

CHAPTER 3

ACTIVITIES OF COLORED MASONS
BEFORE RECEIVING CHARTER

*M*OST WORSHIPFUL John V. De Grasse, P.G.M., of the Prince Hall Grand Lodge of Massachusetts in an address delivered before his Grand Lodge on June 30, 1858, said:

"One year later [1776] according to a statement, which I have in his [Hall's] own handwriting, in company with Thomas Sanderson, Boston Smith [both of whom were made Freemasons with Hall on March 6, 1775] and others, *** he organized and opened, under dispensation granted by this British Travelling Lodge, the first Lodge of Masons composed of Colored men, in America."

On Friday, December 27, 1782, the Lodge celebrated the Feast of St. John, an account of which was printed in a Boston paper on the following Monday by Draper and Folsom, the publishers, in which they referred to the lodge as "St. Blacks" Lodge of Free and Accepted Masons. On the 31st, Hall wrote them a letter on the subject which is signed "Prince Hall, Master of African Lodge, No. 1, Dedicated to St. John."

There are also two letters written to Wor. Bro. William M. Moody, a Master of an English lodge; one dated "Boston, March 2, 1784" and the other "June 30th, 1784; in the year of Masonry 5784." They are both signed by Prince Hall and the second also "In the name of the holle Lodge—C. Underwood, Secretary." Their content is approximately the same. The first was, for many years, believed to be the one Hall sent in order to secure a Warrant, but as the second, which is found in the "Masonic Text Book" by Dr. H. L. Harrison, (Petersburg, Va., 1902) as copied from the Archives in London, has a paragraph not found in the first—namely, "This our humble Petition." etc., it is probable that Wor. Bro. Moody desired the request in this form to secure the Charter and asked for a second letter.

The important point here, though, is that in both letters Hall advises "that this Lodge Hath been founded almost eight years and had no Warrant yet but only a Permet from Grand Master Row (John Rowe, Provincial Grand Master in Boston) to work on St. Johns days and Bury our dead in forme," etc. The first letter did not mention who issued the permit but the second letter distinctly says "Row." This shows that in addition to the Dispensation granted by the Army Lodge, the Provincial Grand Master for all North America—John Rowe, appointed in 1768 by M.˙.W.˙.Brother Beaufort, Grand Master of the Grand Lodge of England (Moderns), gave them a "Permet" to work.

There has been much written concerning the legality with which Hall and his lodge worked during the interim between the time the Army lodge vacated Boston in 1776 and the date of the Charter, 1784, or 1787, when it actually arrived in Boston. There seems little, if any, use in trying to make a case out of such suppositions. In truth we have more evidence of what was going on in African Lodge than we have in the case of many of the most important of the old lodges in the Colonies—several of which appear to have worked without any charter for many years.

It has been usual to consider that while Hall and his Brethren met more or less frequently during the period 1776-1787, they were not "making Masons." In fact the letter of Hall covering the "Permet" appears to eliminate the possibility. On the other hand, the Dispensation from the Army lodge may have permitted such Masonic activity. There are no records to show the periods covered by the Dispensation or the "Permet." There is, however, a record which distinctly sets the whole subject to rest.

"These are a true List of the Living Members of the African Lodge at Present, though there is a number absent at this time." Done "in the Lodge Room, Boston, January 14, 5779 and in the year of our Lord 1779."

The list includes Prince Hall, eighteen Masters, four "Crafts" and eleven Entered Apprentices—thirty-four in all. The officers indicated in the listing are:

*Prince Hall .... *Master*
*Boston Smith .... *Senior Warden*
*Thomas Sanderson .... *Junior Warden*
John Brown .... *Senior Deacon*
George Middleton .... *Junior Deacon*
Scipio Dalton .... *Clerk (Secretary)*
Cato Underwood .... *Steward*
Richard Pollard .... *Marshal*
Pompey Edes (F.C.) .... *Tiler*

*Original members

Of the thirty-four members, seven of the Masters are to be found in the list of those who became Freemasons on March 6, 1775, and one of the Entered Apprentices—Cuff Bufform—is listed. This would indicate that only the Entered Apprentice Degree was conferred on March 6, 1775, or this particular brother only received one degree, as he did not have sufficient financial means to pay for the other two degrees or had to leave before the conferring, if the other two were conferred.

The main point, here, is that out of the fifteen original colored men made Freemasons on March 6, 1775, now (1779) only eight remain in the list of members and yet there are thirty-four members. It is therefore, of necessity that we conclude that either the Lodge was "working," that the other members (i.e. twenty-six of them) are affiliates, or additional colored men were made Freemasons in the Army lodge.

The Lodge has no record of conferring any degrees until 1787, which would indicate that they held to the terms of the "Permet." In fact there has never been a claim that they "worked" until after they received their Charter in 1787.

It may be conceded that Caesar Speer, listed as a "P.M." might be an affiliate, but to believe that the whole twenty-six are affiliates

16

would place four "Crafts" and ten out of the eleven Entered Apprentices in the list of affiliates, which can hardly be probable.

The final conclusion is, then, that the Army lodge made additional Freemasons before it left Castle William, and this can be the only logical answer to the situation.

That the Lodge existed and met during the twelve years between 1775 and 1787 has been demonstrated by documents extant, but there is another part to the document listing the membership, dated January 14, 1779, signed by Hall. It is a list of eight "General Regulations of the African Lodge." Moreover, before the Charter was secured Hall was considered Master of the Lodge—unquestioned as to his right, authority, or legality by the Grand Lodge of England —as shown by a letter written by Wor. Brother Moody on June 21, 1785 to Hall that he had obtained the Charter "in consequence of a letter from the above mentioned lodge, signed by the *then* Master, Prince Hall, and the rest of the officers."

CHAPTER 4

A F R I C A N   L O D G E ,   N O.   4 5 9
I S   C H A R T E R E D

*T*HE first notice we have of an application for a Charter for the Negro brethren is to be found in the two letters to W∴Bro. Moody, cited in the previous Chapter. The two letters are practically identical in respect to words of application. We will excerpt from the June 30th letter, correcting the phonetic spelling:

"We have had no opportunity until now of applying for a Warrant though we were pressed upon to send to France for one but we refused for reasons best known to ourselves. We now apply to the Fountain from which we received light for this favor; and Dear Sir I must beg you to be our advocate for us by sending this, our request, to his Royal Highness the Duke of Cumberland, Grand Master and to the Right Honorable Earl of Effingham, acting Grand Master, the Deputy Grand Master and Grand Wardens and the rest of the Brethren of the Grand Lodge that they would graciously be pleased to grant us a Charter to hold this Lodge as long as we behave up to the spirit of the Constitution.

"This our humble Petition we hope His Highness and the rest of the Grand Lodge will graciously be pleased to grant us there.

"Though poor yet sincere brethren of the craft, and therefor in duty bound, ever to pray, I beg leave to subscribe myself,

> "Your loving Friend and Brother
> "Prince Hall
> "Master of the African Lodge, No. 1"

In Hall's "Letter Book" are a number of letters which explain the delay in getting the Charter. William Gregory, a member of African Lodge, was in London and entrusted with the duty of procuring it.

Prince Spooner, another member of the Lodge was also in London. He wrote to Hall on April 8, 1785, stating that the Charter was still in the office of the Grand Secretary. Gregory had called for it but did not have the fees. In June, 1785, Hall wrote Spooner "as I knew there were on the spot three brothers, I had not the least thought but that they would have paid it." By a ship's steward, a Mr. Hartfield, Hall sent £6-0-8, which Spooner's fee being added, would make the required amount. Hartfield, however, never delivered the money.

Hall next received a letter, dated June 21, 1785, delivered by Captain Washington, a sailing master of Boston, in which Moody advised him he had obtained the Charter—actually issued on September 29, 1784, and that the fee would be 5½ guineas. Hall replied to Moody on August 12, 1785, that "immediately I called the Lodge together and collected twenty dollars and [as] Captain Scott was to sail soon, I had not time to get but a few together." He further requested Spooner to attend to picking up the Charter. Another letter sent on the same date asked him to have Captain Scott bring the Charter on his return trip. Spooner left London before Scott arrived.

On September 22, 1785, Hall wrote the Duke of Cumberland a letter expressing the thanks of the brethren of African Lodge for granting the Charter.

Then came a delay of another year, during which time we have no letters or information to explain it. Hall advised Moody that Captain Scott would advance the money. Scott called directly at the Grand Secretary's office, procured the Charter and Moody advised Hall on March 19, 1787, of the circumstances and that a Book of Constitutions, which Moody had had bound himself, was accompanying the Charter, as a personal gift from him.

Captain Scott delivered the Charter, the Book of Constitutions and a receipt for the fees to Hall on April 29, 1787. The receipt reads as follows:

"Received 28 February 1787, of Captain James Scott, five pounds, fifteen shillings and six pence, being the fee on the

19

Warrant of Constitution of African Lodge at Boston, for the Grand Lodge of the Society of Free and Accepted Masons.
£5-15s-6d   Whm. White, Grand Secretary"

On May 2, 1787, in *The Massachusetts Centinel*, Hall inserted a news item announcing the arrival of the Charter and thanking the members of the fraternity who had "offered the so generous reward in this paper some time since, for the charter supposed to be lost."

The wording of the Charter has been printed many times, but it seems necessary to print it again because of the many errors made by former copyists:

"To all and every:

Our Right Worshipful, Worshipful & loving Brethren: We, Thomas Howard, Earl of Effingham, Lord Howard, etc., etc., etc., Acting Grand Master under the authority of his Royal Highness, Henry Frederick, Duke of Cumberland, etc., etc., etc., Grand Master of the Most Ancient & Honorable Society of Free & Accepted Masons, send Greeting:

"Know Ye That we, at the humble Petition of Our Right Trusty and well beloved Brethren, Prince Hall, Boston Smith, Thomas Sanderson, and several other Brethren residing at Boston, New England, in North America, Do hereby Constitute the said Brethren into a regular Lodge of Free & Accepted Masons, under the Title or Denomination of the African Lodge, to be opened in Boston, aforesaid. And do further, at their said Petition and of the great

Trust and Confidence reposed in each of the said above named Brethren, hereby appoint the said Prince Hall to be Master; Boston Smith, Senior Warden, and Thomas Sanderson, Junior Warden, for the opening of the said Lodge, and for such further time only as shall be thought proper by the Brethren thereof. It being our Will that this, our appointment of the above Officers, shall in no wise affect any future Election of Officers of the Lodge, but that such Election shall be regulated agreeable to such By-Laws of the said Lodge as shall be consistent with the general Laws of the Society, contained in the Book of Constitutions. And we hereby will and require you, the said Prince Hall, to take Special care that all and every the said Brethren are or have been regularly made Masons and that they do observe, perform, and keep all the Rules and Orders contained in the Book of Constitutions. And, further, that you do from time to time cause to be entered in a Book kept for that purpose, an account of your Proceedings in the Lodge, together with all such Rules, Orders, and Regulations as shall be made for the good government of the same; that in no wise you omit once in every Year to send to Us, or our Successors, Grand Masters or to Rowland Holt, Esquire, Our Deputy Grand Master, or to the Deputy Grand Master for the time being, an account in Writing of your said Proceedings and Copies of all such Rules, Orders and Regulations as shall be made as aforesaid, together with A List of the Members of the Lodge, and such Sum of Money as may suit the circumstances of the Lodge, and reasonably be expected towards the Grand Charity. Moreover, we hereby will and require of you, the said Prince Hall, as soon as conveniently may be, to send an Account in Writing of what may be done by virtue of these Presents.

> Given at London, under Our Hand & Seal of Masonry, this 29th Day of Sept. A. L. 5784, A. D. 1784.
> By the Grand Master's Command.

Witness: WM. WHITE, G.S.   [signed] R. HOLT, D.G.M."

I examined the charter in a safe deposit vault in Boston in October, 1931, and found it in a fine state of preservation—only a few words are missing (burned in a fire in 1869 which destroyed a building in Boston where they met. P.G.M. Samuel T. Kendall, at the risk of his life, rescued the Charter). A complete account of the examination was made in the Transactions of the American Lodge of Research, F. & A. M., (N. Y.), Volume I, Number 1, page 65.

The Lodge met under its charter for organization on May 6, 1787 as African Lodge, No. 459, and on May 17, 1787, Hall wrote the Grand Secretary, William White, and acknowledged delivery of the Charter and receipt for fees. He mentioned Hartfield's negligence and advised that he would send a copy of the By-Laws of the Lodge, together with a membership roster. On the same date he wrote a letter to the Deputy Grand Master in which he noted that he had sent the By-Laws and membership list to him. On May 18, Hall wrote to Moody thanking him for his help and for the items which he had sent to the Lodge. He specifically mentioned the bound copy of the Constitutions "which we have shown to some Masters of other Lodges here."

CHAPTER 5

SOME ALLEGED REASONS WHY AFRICAN LODGE IS IRREGULAR

*N*ORMAL procedure is not adequate in relating the historical facts connected with Negro Masonry. For instance, with the original Charter of African Lodge as exhibit "A" and the unquestioned record of its issuance by the Premier Grand Lodge extant, further "discussion" as to the regularity of the lodge would seem super-fluous. But due to a sort of "plague of fear" in the second half of the last century, by nearly all of those who interested themselves in the subject, a number of "excuses for refusing the hand of fellow-ship" were built up and propagated as based on Masonic juris-prudence or fact. As we go along with the story, therefore, it be-comes necessary to take cognizance of some of the more important of these allegations.

In as many cases as possible, no opinion is expressed to dislodge the alleged reasons why the colored brethren are irregular—but simply a citing of similar cases in the annals of the Craft will show the falsity of reasoning by those who have perpetrated such opinions on an unsuspecting public—Masonic or otherwise.

The first protest that we hear is that African Lodge, after the receipt of its Charter, was never constituted or its officers installed. We shall deal with this extremely briefly.

From 1757 to 1810, at least, the "Modern" Grand Lodge of England, which chartered African Lodge, did not require the con-stitution or the installation of the first officers—just as today a Dispensation requires nothing additional to set those named in the document to work as a Lodge, U.D. The very Charter of African Lodge, as well as others issued during the period, reads, "Know ye that we . . . . do hereby *constitute* the said brethren into a regu-lar lodge . . . . hereby appoint the said Prince Hall to be Master;

Boston Smith, Senior Warden; and Thomas Sanderson, Junior Warden, for the opening of said Lodge," etc, etc. Were this not sufficient to clear up this point we would revert to asking a very poignant question, regarding who constituted and/or installed the officers of the Lodge of St. Andrew, Boston; of Independant Royal Arch Lodge, No. 8, now Independent Royal Arch Lodge No. 2; Union Lodge, No. 1, now Mt. Vernon, No. 3, Albany, New York; of The Lodge at Fredericksburg; or of a half dozen others whose records are missing or when extant are entirely silent on this point—to say nothing, in some instances, of inquiring about who even chartered the lodges. We mention these lodges as being in existence now with unquestioned regularity of recognition.

The next matter that has been "bandied about" is that of jurisdiction. When African Lodge was chartered by the "Modern" Grand Lodge of England in 1784, there were three Grand Lodges in that country, each known as the Grand Lodge of England. The lodges in Massachusetts emanating from two of these Grand Lodges were operating as two Provincial Grand Lodges. There was, too, The Lodge of St. Andrew, chartered by the Grand Lodge of Scotland.

It is claimed that the chartering of African Lodge No. 459 was a violation of "territorial jurisdiction"—but whose we have been unable to determine. Up to 1770 the Grand Lodges of the world set up lodges where they saw fit. In that year the Grand Lodges of Holland and England agreed not to charter lodges in the country of each other. This is the first instance of "territorial jurisdiction" recorded. Granting that there were two Grand Lodges in Massachusetts when African Lodge was chartered (which we by no means do, historically), neither of these had exclusive jurisdiction over any particular territory. On Dec. 6, 1782 the "Ancient" Grand Lodge in Massachusetts defined its own jurisdiction, and decreed that no other Grand Lodge could establish lodges in Massachusetts. Such an interdiction was without force, as no agreement had been made with other Grand Lodges, especially with the "Modern" Grand Lodges, and in effect was nothing more than a statement of policy. In 1792 the two Grand Lodges in Massachusetts formed the present Grand Lodge A. F. & A. M. of Massachusetts. This Grand Lodge suggested to the Grand Lodge of New York that it follow the plan of exclusive state jurisdiction. Gradually the various Grand Lodges began to follow such a course and the "American Plan of exclusive Jurisdiction" came into being—but this is by mutual consent and a relinquishment of rights.

As has been stated, the present Grand Lodge of Massachusetts was formed in 1792. It came into being by the union of St. John's ("Modern" Provincial) Grand Lodge of Massachusetts and the "Massachusetts Grand Lodge" of "Ancient" Masons. The latter body "voted that this Grand Lodge be dissolved," in order to accomplish the end in view. Neither of the only two Massachusetts lodges possessing Charters directly from the British Isles (The Lodge of St. Andrew, an "Ancient" lodge, and African Lodge, No. 459, a "Modern" lodge) took part in the formation of the new Grand Lodge. The Lodge of St. Andrew was eagerly sought as a constituent but it refused to become a constituent lodge of the Grand Lodge until 1809. During this period of seventeen years it continued operating under the Grand Lodge of Scotland.

The case of African Lodge, No. 459, is different, however. We have no record that it was ever asked to become a part of the new Grand Lodge at any time—nor of any request by African Lodge— to become affiliated with the Grand Lodge. Hall first applied to become a part of Warren's Provincial Grand Lodge—and later to Rowe, which is probably how he came to secure the "Permet." In 1868, a group of Negro brethren did petition the Grand Lodge of Massachusetts (white) but that was long after the events here related. (See Appendix VI) As it was the only lodge in Massachusetts chartered directly by the "Modern" Grand Lodge, there could be no question as to its Masonic standing, etc. It was simply left out— and we need go no further into the matter of why because there is no *Masonic* reason to justify or explain it. The whole matter was one of social differences.

Some have brought forth the proposition that African Lodge had no further right to exist in Massachusetts after the Grand Lodge of 1792 was formed. There are too many examples of similar "existences" to attempt to call up data on this point. In the first place The Lodge of St. Andrew (shadowy beginning and all) was finally taken into the bosom of the Grand Lodge. In many other states lodges continued under the Grand jurisdiction of their choice for a period of years after the final Grand Lodge was formed. We cite, besides The Lodge of St. Andrew, St. George's Lodge, No. 6, of Schenectady, New York.

CHAPTER 6

THE FIRST NEGRO GRAND LODGE

$\mathcal{O}$N June 24, 1791, a General Assembly of Colored Masons was held at Masons Hall, in the Golden Fleece, Water Street, Boston, where a Grand Lodge was formed, Prince Hall elected Grand Master, and other officers elected and appointed. They were installed by Prince Hall, "assisted by brethren from St. Andrew's Lodge" (white), it has been said, but there is no confirmation of this. It was, in effect, a Provincial Grand Lodge. Grimshaw publishes, in his "Official History of Freemasonry Among the Colored People of North America," a "copy of Dispensation to Prince Hall"—"given under our Hand and Seal of Office at London the 27th day of January, 1791, and Masonry 5791, By the Grand Master's Command, Rawdon, Acting G.M." He says that the document was found among the old manuscripts of African Lodge, No. 459, of Pennsylvania (Peter Richmond, its first secretary) and that there is no doubt that Hall gave them a copy of his authority when he established the lodge in Philadelphia in 1797. The original document has never come to light and the copy was destroyed by fire in Philadelphia, along with numerous other records of the Philadelphia African Lodge. There is no record of the appointment of Hall as a Provincial Grand Master in the archives of the Grand Lodge of England, but neither is there a record there of the appointment of Henry Price, nor of some others who were Provincial Grand Masters. This was the personal prerogative of the Grand Master and not a Grand Lodge matter at that time. Hence many instances are not matters of record in Grand Lodge files.

Whether Hall was actually appointed a Provincial Grand Master or not, he was addressed as a "Right Worshipful" Brother by William White, Grand Secretary of the "Modern" Grand Lodge of England on August 20, 1792, in a letter which requested Hall to investigate the status of a list of lodges constituted by the Grand

27

Lodge of England. The letter also acknowledged the receipt of ten dollars and one guinea for the Charity Fund. Hall replied to the letter as follows:

"I have made inquiry about the Lodges you wrote to me about, the Lodge, No. 42, which used to meet at the Royal Exchange, and kept at the Assembly House, at the head of Orange Tree Lane, has kept a regular Lodge, and was joined last year by one or two other Lodges. Their present Grand Master is John Cutler, chosen last year, and walked to Trinity Church, where a sermon was delivered by Rev. Walter, D.D., June 25th. The Lodge No. 88 hath joined the above Lodge ever since the death of their Grand Master, Henry Price, Esq., for he is long since dead—a worthy Mason. As for Marblehead Lodge, No. 91, I cannot give any information of it, whether it keeps or not; but I believe they don't for if they did, I should have heard from her. As for the Lodge No. 93, in New Haven, Connecticut, I hear they keep a regular Lodge, and I have reason to believe it. The Lodge, No. 142 do keep the same, as some of them hath visited our Lodge, and I heard it from their own mouths.

"I am happy that you approve of the sermon. I have sent you a charge I delivered at Charlestown, on the 25th of June last. I have sent one to your Royal Grand Master, his Royal Highness, the Prince of Wales, and another to his Deputy, and three for the Grand Lodge, which I hope will meet your approval.

Prince Hall"

The first part of this letter speaks for itself. It shows that the Grand Lodge depended upon Hall for its information about the lodges in New England. Also that the white Freemasons were visiting African Lodge. Hall seems to be about the only correspondent in the United States that the English Grand Secretary had at that time.

The second part refers to the pamphlet used as an illustration herewith. This particular copy, as may be seen, belonged to John

His Excellency John Hancock
Robert Morris
#405 — From his Brother
Luther S. Bancroft

CHARGE

Delivered to the Brethren of the

AFRICAN LODGE

On the 25th of June, 1792.

At the Hall of Brother WILLIAM SMITH.

In CHARLESTOWN.

By the Right Worshipful Master

PRINCE HALL.

Printed at the Request of the Lodge.

Printed and Sold at the Bible and Heart, Cornhill, Boston

Title Page of pamphlet by Prince Hall

Hancock and later Rob Morris. It is now owned by the Grand Lodge of New York. Hancock was a brother-in-law of Captain Scott, who brought the original Charter of African Lodge from England, so it is quite natural that he should have had a copy given to him by Hall.

On March 2, 1797, a letter was sent to "Right Worshipful Prince Hall" by Peter Mantore of Philadelphia, the first paragraph of which reads:

"We congratulate you for having been invested with the high and holy trust conferred upon you by the authorities in England, together with your success in obtaining the Warrant constituting African Lodge, 459."

Was the "high and holy trust" a deputation or patent?

On June 15, 1802, Hall wrote a letter to England and gave a list of eight brethren who had died and eighteen who were "entered since 1797."

The "Massachusetts Register," an almanac, published in Boston for a number of years, records the names of Masonic bodies meeting in Massachusetts. In 1806 we find it records African Lodge as meeting on Congress Street, at the home of Prince Hall. Minutes and memoranda in the possession of the Prince Hall Grand Lodge, show meetings of African Lodge from 1787 upwards. From December, 1807 to June, 1846, the lodge held more than four hundred and fifty (450) communications. From 1808 to 1824, at least a hundred and sixteen (116) degrees were conferred on fifty-one (51) candidates.

This (Provincial) Grand Lodge of Colored Masons was formed a year before the present Grand Lodge of Massachusetts (white). When the two Provincial Grand Lodges combined into a single Grand Lodge (white), it is obvious that the third Provincial Grand Body was never taken into consideration in the formation of the new body. The excuse for this, among others, given by historians of the late nineteenth century, was that a single lodge could not form itself into a Grand Lodge. Notwithstanding this view, many of the Provincial Grand Lodges were formed from a single lodge, the first one in Massachusetts being no exception. To take this one pretense for our present purpose, without going into any jurisprudence angles at all, we will simply examine the *modus operandi* of the formation of three Grand Lodges in the United States—not Provincial Grand bodies—as examples of how variations of custom at that time are not now even considered as being irregularities.

The first example is the formation of the Grand Lodge of Tennessee, which came into a separate existence in 1813. Tennessee became a state, separate from North Carolina, on June 1, 1796. In December, 1803, the Grand Lodge of North Carolina, which had carried on in both states, changed its name to include Tennessee. On December 2, 1811, a Convention was held in Knoxville for the purpose of arranging for an independent Grand Lodge for Tennessee. A Committee was formed to present the proposition to the Grand Lodge of North Carolina and Tennessee at the next Annual Communication of that body. On November 21, 1812, the Grand Master, Robert Williams was instructed to prepare a so-called "Great Charter" permitting Tennessee to form a Grand Lodge of the lodges under the jurisdiction of the former Grand Lodge. On December 27, 1813, the Grand Lodge of Tennessee was formed—in effect a "chartered" Grand Lodge.

The second example is the Grand Lodge of New Hampshire. On July 8, 1789, a Convention was held at Portsmouth by "Deputies" from St. John's Lodge at that place and Rising Sun Lodge of Keene, when they voted to establish a Grand Lodge. They then elected Major-General John Sullivan, the most prominent man in the State, Grand Master. He was never Master of his Lodge (St. John's) but this was speedily corrected by making him the Master of the Lodge. On July 16, 1789, twelve brethren from these two lodges and St. Patrick's Lodge met in a second Convention and transacted some further business. On January 27, 1790 six brethren attended a third Convention. On April 8, 1790, in the presence of thirty-one brethren the Grand Master and officers of the Grand Lodge were installed. Thus was the Grand Lodge of New Hampshire established.

The third example is the Grand Lodge of New Jersey. On December 18, 1786 a group of twenty-six Masons, acting individually, met in New Brunswick and drew up a memorial nominating seven Freemasons, one, the Grand Master-nominate, never signing the document, as officers *pro temp.* to continue in office "till the anniversary of St. John the Evangelist," 1787. After adjourning, seven others signed the document and on January 30, 1787, seventeen others—a total of fifty—also attached their signatures to it. Twenty-three were members of Lodge No. 10 at Baskingridge; one from St. John's No. 1, Newark; four from Lodge, No. 32, at Burlington, New Jersey Lodges. These totalled twenty-eight of the members. The others were ten from Pennsylvania; five from New York; two from Lodge, No. 190, South Carolina; two from England; one from Massachusetts; and two unknown, making the additional twenty-two members signing.

On January 30, 1787, thirty-eight brethren were present at New Brunswick and the Grand Master "elect" was installed by "the oldest Master Mason present, then Master of a Lodge," Wor. Brother William McKissack, M.D. of Lodge, No. 10. He then installed the rest of the officers. When or where the M.∴W.∴Grand Master, Lt.-Col. David Brearley, Chief Justice of the Supreme Court of New Jersey was made a Mason is not known. Neither is there any reference to his ever having been a Master of a lodge. Five Dispensations for lodges, good for three months, were issued. The point we wish to bring out is that these individual Masons formed a Grand Lodge without representing their respective lodges. In fact only two of the lodges whose members participated in forming the Grand Lodge of New Jersey received Dispensations to hold a lodge, numbers 10 and 1. Yet this grand body immediately became the body of dispensation, and shortly later chartered the Masonic lodges of New Jersey. Its legality or regularity has never been questioned.

As a matter of fact the English Grand Lodges of 1717 and 1751 were formed by the "Assembly" method, which Hall also used.

As to the citing of cases of one lodge becoming a "Mother" Lodge or Grand Lodge, there are so many in the history of the Craft that we shall simply enumerate a few without even going into their history. The Lodge at Kilwinning, Scotland; the English Lodge at Bordeaux, France; the The "Three Globes" at Berlin, Germany; etc, etc.

CHAPTER 7

LODGES CHARTERED BY PRINCE HALL

𝒯HE first lodge growing out of the African Grand Lodge was in Philadelphia, Pennsylvania. Peter Mantore wrote a letter to Prince Hall, dated March 2, 1797, asking "for a Dispensation for an African Lodge." He says "We have been tried by five Royal Arch Masons. The White Masons have refused to give us a Dispensation, fearing that black men living in Virginia would get to be Masons, too." He advised that there were eleven, of which five were Masters—and he named them, as follows:

Peter Mantore, Acting Master—elevated a Super-excellent, and was Arch and Royal Arch Knight Templar of Ireland, Carricfergus Lodge, True Blues, No. 253.

Peter Richmond
Jonathan Harding
John Davis
Robert Vendbel
} Masters—Ancient York Masons.

Q. Butler
C. Brown
T. Peterson
J. Tucker
J. Daking
J. Henry
} Made in London in the Golden Lodge, No. 22

The letter shows that they tried to get a Dispensation from the white Masons in Philadelphia. Israel Israel, a member of Royal Arch Lodge, No. 3, in Philadelphia (M.M. May 20, 1794 and G.M. of Pa. 1803 - 1805) visited this lodge in 1797 and reported its existence to his Grand Lodge (minutes of March 6, 1797).

Hall's reply, dated March 22, 1797 is as follows:

"I received your letter of the 2 which informed me that there are a number of blacks in your city who have received the light of masonry, and I hope they got it in a just and lawful manner. If so, dear brother, we are willing to set you at work under our charter and Lodge, No. 459, from London; under that authority, and by the name of the African Lodge, we hereby and herein give you license to assemble and work as aforesaid, under that denomination as in the sight and fear of God. I would advise you not to take any in at present till your officers and your Master be in[stalled] in the Grand Lodge, which we are willing to [do] when he thinks convenient, and he may receive a full warrant instead of a permit.

Prince Hall."

A warrant was granted on June 24, 1797 and on September 22nd the lodge was formally constituted as African Lodge, No. 459, of Philadelphia, by Prince Hall. Absolom Jones, first colored Priest in the Episcopal Church of America, was Master. Richard Allen, founder and first Bishop of the African Methodist Episcopal Church, was first Treasurer.

The second lodge which Hall set to work was Hiram Lodge, No. 3, in Providence, Rhode Island, composed of some members of the Boston Lodge who lived in Rhode Island. It was warranted on June 25, 1797, the day following the warranting of the Philadelphia lodge. About 1813 most of the members of the lodge migrated to Liberia with the settlement project of the African Humane Society and the lodge finally became dormant.

These two instances of the chartering of lodges are the only "official acts" of Prince Hall during his Grand Mastership, except his veto of a proposed change of name of the Philadelphia Lodge. On April 18, 1792, the Grand Lodge of England renumbered the lodges on its Register. The Proceedings of that Grand Lodge of November 21, 1792 give the new numbers. African Lodge in Boston became No. 370.

34

CHAPTER 8

THE PRINCE HALL GRAND LODGE

$\mathcal{S}$IX MONTHS after Prince Hall died, a delegate convention of Negro Masons was held in Boston—July 24, 1808—with representatives of the lodges at Boston, Philadelphia and Providence present. The Deputy Grand Master, Nero Prince, a Russian Jew, was elected Grand Master and the name of the Grand Lodge was changed to "Prince Hall Grand Lodge" in honor of their former leader and first Grand Master.

Nero Prince served as Grand Master for two years. He left this country some time in 1810 and returned to Russia the following year. Grimshaw says "he died in 1825 at the age of 87, and was buried in the Lutheran Chapel Cemetery, Moscow."

The third Grand Master was George Middleton, whose name is listed as a member of African Lodge in the roster of 1779. He also served two years. He granted a warrant for Union Lodge, No. 2 in Philadelphia.

From 1811 to 1817, Peter Lew was Grand Master. He warranted Laurel Lodge, No. 5 and Phoenix Lodge, No. 6, in 1811 in Philadelphia. On February 16, 1812, Boyer Lodge, No. 1, in New York, was also warranted.

Thus we have the original African Lodge warranted by the Grand Lodge of England; two lodges warranted by Prince Hall as Grand Master of African Grand Lodge before 1808; and at least four lodges warranted by the Prince Hall Grand Lodge, prior to December 27, 1813, when the two Grand Lodges of England combined into the present United Grand Lodge of England.

One of the strongest attacks against the regularity of Prince Hall Masonry by the "recognized" bodies of Freemasonry has been that the Grand Lodge of England "wiped" out the African Lodge, No. 370, in 1813 by removing it from its Register. To this, however, we cannot subscribe.

In the first place, at the reorganization of the colored Grand Lodge in 1808, the title specifically shows it to be a "Grand Lodge of Massachusetts," and thus an independent Grand Body. We consider it legally formed, too. Therefore, if it is considered that all that went before 1813 was regular, as those who propose this "wiping" off the Register do, then nothing which the United Grand Lodge of England could do would effect the status of the Grand Lodge or the Lodge itself, then a constituent of the Prince Hall Grand Lodge of Massachusetts.

However, for those who cannot take that view, we shall examine the action of the United Grand Lodge of England and see just what had taken place when it published the revised list of its lodges for the first time on March 2, 1814.

The "Moderns" had, in 1813, five hundred and sixty-eight lodges on their list, including the Grand Steward's Lodge. The Athol or "Ancients" at the same time had three hundred and forty lodges on their list. When the pruning was finished the lists looked thus:

	1813	Erased	Remaining
Moderns	568	181	387
Ancients	340	80	260
	———	———	———
Total	908	261	647

Of those erased in the United States they were as follows:

Moderns		Ancients	
Conn.	1	N. Y.	4
Ga.	3	Pa.	2
Md.	1	S. C.	3
Mass.	4		—
Mich.	3	Total	9
N. Y.	3		
N. C.	2		
R. I.	1		
S. C.	6		
Va.	4		
	—		
Total	28		

Thus South Carolina had 9 and N. Y. 7 lodges erased.

The lodges erased fall into two classes: One, those whose existence had been terminated by dormancy and, two, lodges then under the aegis of some Grand Lodge in the United States.

Let us look at the example of South Carolina. In 1776, the Provincial Grand Lodge dissolved itself and became an independent Grand Lodge. In 1787 five "Ancient" lodges formed a rival Grand Lodge and these two Grand Lodges combined on February 18, 1818, the date of the first meeting after the "union." Thus South Carolina lodges (six "Modern" and three "Ancient"), if extant, were already under one of the two independent Grand Lodges then existing.

African Lodge was already a constituent of an independent Grand Lodge in Massachusetts and likewise was erased—as was every other extant lodge in the United States on the Register of the two Grand Lodges of England at the time of the union.

African Lodge had among its members some affiliates who were made Freemasons in Europe under the "Ancient" system, which included the Royal Arch Degree. Some of the other members of the lodge desired to receive this degree also. As their charter did not permit the conferring of other than the three symbolic degrees, some of the members—as individuals—petitioned the United Grand Lodge of England on January 5, 1824, about the matter (the letter is printed in the Proceedings of the Grand Lodge of Massachusetts [white] for 1870, page 49). As there was a Negro Royal Arch Chapter in Philadelphia which had been operating since 1820, that may have been another reason why the Boston brethren desired to have authority to confer the degree. The "Modern" English Grand Lodge never gave authority to confer the Royal Arch Degree and while the degree was recognized after the Union, probably upon the insistance of the "Ancients," the Grand Lodge continued its policy not to include the right to confer it in their lodges. But, the Grand Lodge of England no longer considered itself as having any kind of authority over the lodges in the United States, as all were dropped from its Register in 1813.

On June 18, 1827, the Prince Hall Grand Lodge of Massachusetts declared its position publicly by publishing in a Boston newspaper that they "declare themselves free and independent of any Lodge from this day and that we will not be tributary or be governed by any Lodges than that of our own."

From 1791, when Prince Hall became Grand Master, down to the present there have been a regular succession of Grand Masters, the list showing forty-nine down to 1939.

CHAPTER 9

THE NATIONAL GRAND LODGE

*I*N THE natural course of events the Prince Hall Grand Lodge of Massachusetts chartered lodges in the nearby states and these soon began to form Grand Lodges in the same manner as the white Grand Lodges. The second Grand Lodge to be formed was that of Pennsylvania on December 27, 1815. The third, however, did not come along until thirty years later. This was New York— and Maryland followed the same year. In Appendix I will be found the dates of the formation of all the Negro Grand Lodges.

During the progress of Negro Freemasonry a body was formed which caused dissension among the ranks and impeded the growth and strength which the Negro bodies had been gaining in the United States. This was the National Compact Grand Lodge of North America. It's formation grew out of a small circumstance in the State of Pennsylvania promoted by some unscrupulous white men.

In 1828, Harmony Lodge, No. 5 of Philadelphia, working under the First Independent African Grand Lodge of Pennsylvania, had its charter revoked, being charged with contumacy. In 1833 the members of the expelled lodge applied for a charter through some lodge in Norristown, which was supposedly working under a charter from the Grand Lodge of Ohio (white). For a consideration of money ($125.00—half of which was paid by Union Lodge, No. 4, also expelled by the First Independent African Grand Lodge) they were given a charter dated May 7, 1833, and organized under their original name, Harmony Lodge, No. 5. Shortly afterward, Union Lodge, No. 4, appeared to be working under this same "authority" together with at least two other lodges to which Harmony Lodge, No. 5, granted dispensations. On July 17, 1837 representatives of these lodges met in Philadelphia and organized a body known as the Hiram Grand Lodge of Pennsylvania, in opposition to the First Independent African Grand Lodge.

The Hiram Grand Lodge continued to function for about ten years but the differences between it and the First Independent African Grand Lodge caused continued dissension among the Negro Masons in Pennsylvania.

In the June 18, 1845, issue of the "Public Ledger" of Philadelphia, a rather lengthy item appeared—being the report of a Committee of the First Independent African Grand Lodge which showed that the Grand Lodge of Ohio (white) never met in Chillicothe, Ohio, where the Harmony Lodge, No. 5 charter was reputed to have been granted; and that the Mayor of Chillicothe, one William H. Skerrett a member of Scioto Lodge, No. 6, of that town, and an officer of it for more than twenty years, signed a document certifying the same.

On the June 20th following, an answer from the Hiram Grand Lodge in the same paper simply reiterated the facts of its manner of securing the charter.

Then, in the "Masonic Review" of Cincinnati, Ohio, May, 1847, a circular was published, dated Columbus, April 7, 1847, signed by the Grand Master of the Grand Lodge of Ohio (white), which denied that that Grand Lodge had any lodge by the name of Harmony, No. 5 on its Register; that it met in Chillicothe on the charter date or any other for the fifteen years previous; that it had any lodges at all in Pennsylvania or even any State where there was already a Grand Lodge; and that it ever had any of the officers named on the charter as members of Grand Lodge.

Although this should have silenced the Hiram Grand Lodge it only added fuel to the fire because this newly created body had grown in membership and power, whereas the original Grand Lodge had decreased in membership and was losing its once unchallenged position in the Negro Craft in Pennsylvania. In fact, it feared for its very life.

In an effort to clear up the situation, and to bring a closer union among the Negro Masons of the United States, M∴W∴John T. Hilton, Grand Master of the Prince Hall Grand Lodge of Massachusetts, called together delegates from the two Pennsylvania Grand

Lodges, his own Grand Lodge and the Boyer Grand Lodge of New York, to meet in Boston on June 23, 1847.

There is much controversy as to just what took place during this day and the three following, as well as a fifth day, the 28th of June. It is claimed that only the Massachusetts Grand Lodge and the Hiram Grand Lodge of Pennsylvania were present on the first day; that no meeting was held on the second, but a celebration; that on the next two days a General Grand Lodge was formed, with or without the presence of some of the delegates. At any rate some time during the week a body was formed which became generally known as the National Compact Grand Lodge, whose subsequent actions showed it to have defeated the very idea of the "get-together" because it created more havoc in the Negro Craft than the Pennsylvania bodies could ever have done, in or out of their own State.

When the delegates of the Boyer Grand Lodge (Prince Hall) of New York, returned and reported that they had agreed to the action of the Boston convention, the Boyer body repudiated the agreement. This act caused a schism and those who withdrew established a National Compact Grand Lodge on October 12, 1848. Then followed a schism in Pennsylvania with another Grand Lodge being set up there. Similar actions occurred in other States.

A complete recording of the activities of the National Compact Grand Lodge would constitute a volume of considerable proportions. The full name of the body and a record of its meetings will be found in the Appendix. Over a period of thirty years it continued to exist when, in 1877, it was formally dissolved. After that three or four unscrupulous brethren, using the good names of some of the former National Grand Masters as "bait", did succeed in making Masons, clandestinely, and setting up a few lodges in five or six States—but they were so fully exposed in 1890 that nothing of consequence was thereafter heard about their activities.

A collection of the addresses and memorials against the organization would likewise fill a large volume. The ramifications of the effect of the National Compact Grand Lodge upon Negro Masonry of the United States can only be compared with the effect upon the

Craft that the Scottish Rite controversy, in the middle of the last century, had upon white Masonry. The full story of either will probably never be pieced together.

The "National Compact" Grand Lodge in New York, issued a charter for a Regimental Lodge in 1864. As it is the only known charter of its kind in existence that was issued during the Civil War, it is herewith reproduced.

Alexander H. Newton was in Company E, John Andrews was in Company D and Richard Giles in Company H of the 29th Connecticut Colored Infantry. A full military record may be found in the office of the Adjutant General at Hartford, Connecticut.

Samuel J. Scottron, who signed the charter as Grand Secretary, p.t., was a well known Brooklyn, New York resident, and is identified with the "Compact" movement as one of its leaders. Nothing is known as to the possible activities of the lodge.

A few other Negro regimental lodges are known to have existed, one being in the 55th Massachusetts Volunteer Militia at Fort Wagner. More recently military lodges have been carried on the rolls of several of the Prince Hall Grand Lodges. In 1920 the Grand Lodge of Missouri had three on its Register, Malta Military Lodge, No. 138, Fort Huachuca, Arizona; Tyre Military Lodge, No. 143, Columbus, New Mexico; and Joppa Military Camp Lodge, No. 150, Stotsenberg Camp, Pampanga, Philippine Islands.

REGIMENTAL WARRANT.

To all whom it may concern :

WISDOM, STRENGTH AND STABILITY.

I, *David Gorden*, Most Worshipful Grand Master for the State of New York and Masonic Jurisdiction thereunto belonging, and National Masonic Union.

Having received a petition from the members of the 29th United States Colored Troops, praying for a Charter, to empower them to meet as a Lodge of Free Masons in said Regiment, to work according to the ancient Constitution, laws, and usages of Freemasonry, according to the ancient York Rite, and they, the said members of the above named Regiment, having to my satisfaction been well recommended.

I do, by virtue of the power in me vested, grant this as their Lawful Warrant, so long as they, the said members, shall conform to all the laws and usages of the Order, empowering them to work in their Regiment and nowhere else, and in no manner whatever to interfere with the rights of any established Lodge or Grand Lodge.

Furthermore, I do appoint our worthy and beloved brother *Alex. H. Newton* to be the Worshipful Master: *John Andrews*, Senior Warden, and *Richard Giles*, Junior Warden of said Lodge, to be called and known by the name and title of

PHŒNIX LODGE NO. 1.

And I do furthermore authorize and empower our said worthy and beloved brethren, to admit and make Free Masons, according to the most ancient, and honorable custom of the royal craft, so long as the above named Regiment shall remain together as such, and not longer, and on the return of the Regiment, this warrant shall be deposited with the most worshipful Grand Master for the State of New York.

Now, Brethren, we do command you, and your successors in office, to make regular quarterly returns to the Grand Master of all work done, with your tax and assessments for the same.

Now, by the grace of God, I, *David Gorden* Most Worshipful Grand Master for the State of New York, and Masonic jurisdiction thereunto belonging, do, by the power and authority to me committed, sign this warrant and cause the great seal of the Most Worshipful Grand Lodge to be here affixed this *18th* day of *March* A.D. 1864, A.L. 5864.

Attest.

David Gorden M. W. G. M.

Samuel J. Scottron M. W. G. S. Pro Tem.

Warrant granted by "Compact Grand Lodge" of New York for a Negro Military Lodge during Civil War

CHAPTER 10

WHITE GRAND LODGES CONSIDER NEGRO FREEMASONRY

*I*N MOST of the jurisdictions the white Grand Lodges, at various times, have had the subject of Negro Masonry brought upon the floor of Grand Lodge. The reasons have been many and varied but usually it was because of some phase of recognition.

Let us take the Grand Lodge of New York as an instance. In the Proceedings of this Grand Lodge for October 7, 1818, the Grand Lodge was called into special session to consider a "Masonic Notice" which had appeared in the newspapers. The notice was dated October 2nd, and was signed by one Wm. Sandy Lattion, and called for a meeting of "those belonging to African Lodge of Free and Accepted Masons." A Committee was appointed to inquire into the matter and they reported on March 3, 1819. Nothing further came of it. The group was no doubt Boyer Lodge, warranted in 1812 by the Prince Hall Grand Lodge of Massachusetts. In the Proceedings of March 4, 1829, we find R.˙.W.˙.Elias Hicks reporting for a Committee on investigating Boyer Lodge, No. 1, in which said lodge is denounced as clandestine. On June 6, 1845, a memorial was presented to Grand Lodge from Boyer Lodge, No. 1, praying for recognition. The Proceedings of June 2, 1846, go into further detail on the matter but report as in 1829.

In 1868 the matter of recognizing Negro Masonry came to the attention of the Grand Lodge of Massachusetts (white), although it was the outgrowth of an entirely different subject. This was not the first time that the subject of recognizing Negro Masons was brought upon the floor of this Grand Lodge. However, the extended report made upon the subject this time by M.˙.W.˙.William S. Gardner has been used by many other Grand Lodges when they had to deal with the same subject. An examination of the report will show that it will not withstand the test of the "square and level."

In 1875, the Grand Lodge of Ohio investigated the matter of Negro Masonry and an even more extended report than that of M.·. W.·.Brother Gardner was made by a Committee previously mentioned in Chapter II. The result of the presentation of this report was a parliamentary quibble in which the subject at hand was completely lost sight of, and never brought before Grand Lodge again.

In 1897, the Grand Lodge of Washington, after an investigation by a Committee, accorded quasi-recognition to colored Freemasons, in that they allowed lodges to receive visitors from the Negro Grand Lodges, should they, in their judgement, think fit so to do. This caused a storm of protest throughout the Grand Lodges of the United States (white), most of whom looked into the subject from whatever angle that suited their convenience. From October, 1898, to June, 1899, sixteen Grand Lodges severed fraternal intercourse with the Grand Lodge of Washington—but before May, 1900, seven of these had again "recognized" Washington, and finally all resumed fraternal relations.

These are the cases which are most frequently discovered by those who read the older Proceedings of Grand Lodges. There are many others.

Nothing of a practical nature, however, has ever come out of any of the attempts toward recognition of Negro Freemasons by white Grand Lodges, and the status of Negro Freemasonry remains much as it did in the early last century. It is left to its own devices so completely that the white Freemason knows practically nothing whatever of the extent of its activities. Thousands of white Freemasons have never heard of a Negro Freemason in the United States and what few do come in contact with them give the matter little thought. Consequently it is a great shock when they discover that out of every eight Freemasons in the country, one is a Negro.

One thing about the attempts of recognition of Negro Freemasons by white Grand Lodges has always been lost sight of. Since 1850, including the three instances above mentioned, they were not instigated by the Negro brethren but by white brethren. Prince Hall Masons have not sought to alter the existing status of their relations with white Freemasons themselves. Liberals among the Craft have always been responsible for bringing the matter to the attention of the various white Grand Lodges where it has reached the floor of these bodies.

CHAPTER 11

SYMBOLIC FREEMASONRY
AMONG NEGROES TODAY

*T*HERE is a Negro Grand Lodge in each of thirty-seven States, the District of Columbia and in Ontario, Canada. In Idaho, Maine, Montana, Nevada, New Hampshire, North Dakota, Oregon, South Dakota, Utah, Vermont and Wyoming, where no Grand Lodges of Negro Freemasons exist, there are only 5,917 male Negroes (1930 census). Although a number of these are Freemasons, and several lodges have been formed in these States, it has not been deemed feasible to form Grand Lodges.

During the period 1929-30, an estimate of the number of Negro Freemasons in the United States would be about three quarters of a million and the number of lodges between five and six thousand. Accurate statistics are not available to properly enumerate the number of members or lodges, but the present membership is probably not over a half million. Proceedings of Negro Grand Lodges are difficult to secure and even when they are found full statistics are often not included.

The lodges and Grand Lodges operate on the same general plan as the "recognized" Grand Lodges (white) in the United States. Their whole physical set-up is similar to the operations and activities of the white brethren. The "work" is likewise similar, as they derive from the Grand Lodge of England. There are differences in the work among their Grand jurisdictions, just as in the white Grand Lodges, but the work does not differ from the latter any more than between Grand Lodges of the same. Like their white brethren they have come to adopt the "American Plan of Exclusive State Jurisdiction" for themselves.

Some of the Negro Grand Lodges, especially that of Ohio, have been recognized by Grand Lodges outside of the United States, and some of these same Grand Lodges have been recognized by white Grand Lodges in this country.

We have dwelt, in the past pages, particularly on the early years of Freemasonry among Negroes in the United States, when matters have to be judged in the light of what was common practice at that time. Present-day Masonic practices cannot be used to gage what took place in these early years. This has been the common error made by most historians or committees in considering Negro Masonry. After the establishment of the first few lodges and Grand Lodges, the fraternity grew among the Negroes to its present state as white Freemasonry has done. There seems little use in covering these later periods at all in the present undertaking. From the start of the Grand Lodge in each State, a separate history should be written for the brethren of each particular State.

We have tried to show, by logical reasoning, that Negro Freemasonry in this country has a legal and proper beginning and that it has carried on in the same manner. That it is not recognized by the white Grand Lodges is not because of anything it did but rather because of an entirely different reason which "White Freemasonry," to give it such a term, has not been honest enough to frankly state—the presence of a social system peculiar to this country. Freemasonry is a social institution, among other things. Our social system separates colored from white people.

Each Grand Lodge, as set up in the United States, determines for itself what shall constitute a basis for recognition. After a Grand Lodge has been found to conform with recognition requirements, it then becomes a matter for Grand Lodge to grant or refuse recognition according to its pleasure. We cannot see how any Committee, qualified to examine the subject of Negro Masonry, by being fully versed in the history, jurisprudence and irregularities of "recognized" Freemasonry in the United States, especially during the early periods of the organized Craft, could but recommend recognition from a *Masonic* standpoint. In fact more than once, as we have pointed out, has this been done. The reasons why the Grand Lodges of Negro Freemasonry have not been recognized, then, must be found outside of the Masonic sphere. These reasons are social ones. The Negro Freemasons have not been recognized because they are

Negroes. It is neither a question of purely Masonic nature or only one of color. It is based on the social system of this country and thus it will rest until the system is changed.

CHAPTER 12

WHITE BRETHREN IN
PRINCE HALL LODGES

*W*E WILL enumerate just a few of the many cases of white brethren in colored Prince Hall bodies. They are recorded more as a matter of interest rather than a recital of historical facts. One or two side-lights are also presented.

CARTHAGINIAN LODGE, No. 47 (P.H.) Brooklyn, N. Y.

In 1905, Frederick M. Holzworth, born of German parentage, resided at 443 Waverly Ave., Brooklyn, N. Y. He was elected on June 29, 1905 in Carthaginian Lodge, No. 47 (P.H.) He received his Entered Apprentice Degree on October 3rd; his Fellowcraft on November 21st; and his Master Mason Degree on December 5th, of the same year. A photograph of him, together with other members of the lodge, taken in 1909, is extant. He later moved to Huntington, New York, but he continued his membership in the lodge until his death a few years ago.

EL SOL DE CUBA LODGE, No. 38 (P.H.) New York, N. Y.

This was a Spanish-speaking lodge of colored men. In 1908-1910 eighteen men of Italian parentage were made Master Masons in the lodge and eight others became Fellowcrafts. Some time later these brethren became aware of the difference between the white and colored lodges and, one by one, with the fraternal blessing of the lodge, they withdrew. Some became members of Italian Lodges in the city. We have the names of all of these brethren and the record is extant in the minutes of the lodge. At the time of this happening the late Arthur A. Schomburg (died June 17, 1938) noted scholar and Curator of the Division of Negro Literature, History and Prints of the New York Public Library, was Secretary of the Lodge. It is now Prince Hall Lodge, No. 38, English speaking, because most of the older members returned to Cuba or Porto Rico following the war in 1898.

EUREKA LODGE, No. 11 (P.H.) Savannah, Georgia

In the archives of the Grand Lodge of Georgia is a record of the first initiations held in this lodge, chartered January 4, 1866. One Miller Max, a white man, and a member of Clinton Lodge, No. 54, in Savannah, occupied the station of Junior Steward during the first initiation. Later three other white brethren were members of the lodge. One, who secured a demit, later became a member of a Wisconsin lodge and finally affiliated with Clinton, No. 54.

DOWNSHIRE LODGE, No. 12, (P.H.) New York, N. Y.

A number of white members of this lodge became members of Shakespeare Lodge, No. 750 (white) during the period between the time of Dispensation, February 10, 1874, and the time it received its Charter, June 5, 1874. There is considerable information that might be presented regarding this circumstance, but, like the other cases, it is simply noted here as a happening. (The entire membership of this lodge was white, with the exception of the Secretary, Albert Wilson, who was a Negro).

MICHIGAN INCIDENT

In the Proceedings of the Grand Lodge of Michigan (P.H.) there is a curious item covering an incident of a white applicant of good repute who was rejected by Granite Lodge, No. 11 (P.H.). It seems that the members had been canvassed and had agreed not to reject him. When the agreement was not kept the Master reported it to his Grand Lodge with the hope of getting some relief—but, of course, he was not successful.

NEW YORK—NORTH CAROLINA INCIDENT

Paul Drayton, who was born in the Carolinas, was the first Grand Master of the Negro Grand Lodge of New York. Later he became National Grand Master of the National Compact Grand Lodge. In 1865 he assisted in establishing a lodge in New Berne, North Carolina. The Grand Lodge (white) of North Carolina, believing it was the Grand Lodge of New York (white) "invading" its jurisdiction, protested. In 1866 two letters were received from individuals in North Carolina by the Grand Secretary of the Grand Lodge of New York (white) which will be found in the Appendix.

The Proceedings of the Grand Lodge of North Carolina (white) of 1865 and 1866 record the results of investigations into the matter.

A RECENT INCIDENT—ETHIOPIAN SUPREME COUNCIL FOR THE UNITED STATES

At the 73rd Congress of the United States, Second Session, on January 9, 1934, a Bill (H.R. 6620) was introduced in the House of Representatives entitled, "Incorporating the National Ethiopian Supreme Council of the Universal Order of Free Masons (Ethiopian Rites Inclusive)." The Bill stated that "James Cannon be the first eminent grand master, Maawad Saadallah, the first grand secretary, Richard A. Carr, the first deputy grand master," of the proposed body. It was sent to Committee but never reported back to the House.

In 1922 this same James Cannon, who signed himself "Hon. James Cannon," Grand Master of New York and New Jersey, of "Grand Lodge, No. 1, A.F. & A.M., Long Branch, N. J.," entered into a controversy with one Abdul Hamid Suleiman, 1° to 96°, who claimed Arabian Masonry as his forte. The above mentioned Bill was an outgrowth of this controversy. A private investigation of the representation of Cannon was made in 1922 in India, where he claimed to have received his authority, and also in 1934 additional investigations were made of some new "information" about his claims but all of the representations proved to be without foundation.

The literature of Negro Freemasonry is replete with many items such as listed above. Rt. Wor. Brother Harry A. Williamson, P.D. G.M. (P.H.) of New York, has made a bibliography of articles written on Negro Masonry. It comprises 1443 separate items and has taken nearly a life-time to prepare. Needless to say it is a source of great value to historians of Negro Masonry.

CHAPTER 13

CHAPTER, COUNCIL AND COMMANDERY

*T*HESE three bodies of Freemasonry have their counterpart in Negro Masonry. Their derivation, however, is not at all clear and very little is known regarding the manner of their origin among the Negro Freemasons. As their origin among white Freemasons is clouded to a great degree, it is hardly to be expected that the appearance of the degrees among colored brethren would be otherwise. Very little, except a few generalities, has been written on the subject of degrees and Orders outside of the symbolic lodge in connection with colored Freemasonry. Grimshaw had a Chapter on the "Origin of Royal Arch Masons" and one on "Knights Templars Among Colored Men" in his book, but no mention of Cryptic Masonry is to be found.

Regarding Royal Arch Masonry he says, "In 1774 Passey Benjamine, Rev. Peter Mantore, Caesar Worthington and Caesar Thomas, from Martinique, French West Indies; James Forten, Thomas Depee, Robert Bogle, Jonathan Harding, Mark Stevenson, Nathan Gray, William Jeffers, Robert Barclay, Peter Richmond and Richard Nurse, natives of Haiti, and other seafaring men, received all the degrees of Freemasonry, including that of Knighthood, and certificates from St. George Lodge, No. 32, Liverpool, and St. John's Lodge, No. 80, London, England, where they were made Masons. These fifteen Brethren settled in Philadelphia, Pa., in 1776, and became active and useful citizens."

Grimshaw then says that in 1776 eleven colored Freemasons, seven of whom are named above, and five others, not listed, together with "others, obtained from Provincial Grand Master George Harris a dispensation to organize a lodge of Royal Arch Masons which was granted March 18th, 1776. At this time war between the colonies and Great Britain prevented them from organizing until

October 12th, 1820, when Union Chapter of Royal Arch Masons was established, with Caesar Thomas, High Priest, and other officers; Chapter No. 3 (white) of Philadelphia, Pa., assisting in the work."

As this account is the only one *"in extenso"* in any work on Negro Masonry, and as there are no data extant to give us the facts, we will simply have to examine what we have to see if it can be taken "as is" or in part, until further evidence comes to light regarding the beginning of Capitular Masonry among the Negro Brethren in the United States.

We have quoted the names given by Grimshaw because it is necessary to refer to Chapter VII and compare them with the names in Peter Mantore's letter to Prince Hall on March 2, 1797. In this letter Mantore stated he received his various degrees, including Royal Arch, in Carricfergus Lodge, True Blues, No. 253, Ireland. In the present instance Grimshaw lists the Lodges No. 32 in Liverpool and No. 80 in London. Peter Richmond and Jonathan Harding in the letter are listed as "Master—Ancient York Masons" with no lodge of "raising" being mentioned. Then, again, so far as all of those listed as receiving their degrees in lodges No. 32 and No. 80, are concerned in 1774—St. George, No. 32, in Liverpool, was not warranted until May 30, 1786, and St. John's, No. 80, in London, not until December 18, 1805. The degrees could not have been conferred in them twelve and thirty-one years previously. It really makes no difference where they did receive their degrees so far as the final legalizing is concerned, but we hope, some day, to be able to discover this information.

That George Harison was meant when "George Harris" is mentioned by Grimshaw cannot be seriously doubted. But there are four extremely odd circumstances to overcome before we can believe that Harison would or did grant a dispensation to organize a "lodge of Royal Arch Masons" on March 18, 1776. The first is that there is no record of Harison chartering any lodges of Royal Arch Masons —and only a couple of lodges which conferred the Royal Arch Degree are associated in any way with his authorizations—but by no means proved, as yet.

The second is that it seems very strange that having a dispensation for a lodge in which they could confer the Royal Arch Degree in 1776, that in 1797 this same man, and some of the others then listed, applied to Prince Hall for "an African Lodge after having been refused by the Philadelphia 'white Masons'."

Thirdly, we are told that the dispensation lay dormant until October 12, 1820—forty-four years later—when Caesar Thomas was made High Priest of the newly organized "Union Chapter." The dispensation, Grimshaw says, was for a "lodge of Royal Arch Masons" but it appears that a "Chapter" was formed. Caesar Thomas, if he was made a Freemason in 1774, as related, could be no less than sixty-seven (67) years of age at this time (1820) and would, more than likely have been over seventy (70) years old.

The fourth reason precludes any further discussion in the matter. George Harison died on April 18, 1773, three years before Grimshaw says he issued the Charter. There seems little doubt that this Chapter was formed in 1820, however. In 1826, a second Chapter was formed (Jerusalem) and in 1844 a third (Friendship). These three Chapters organized in the latter year a Grand Chapter, The First Independent African Grand Chapter of North America, with Jacob Jenkins as Grand High Priest, with headquarters in Philadelphia. There is a minute book of Prudence Chapter, No. 5 in Philadelphia recording Convocations from May 2, 1848 to Sept. 4, 1869. Royal Arch Masonry has now spread, from this first Grand Chapter, into other States and most of them have Grand Chapters of their own working along the same lines as the white Grand and subordinate Chapters.

As to Cryptic Masonry among the Negro brethren, we find the first mention by the late William T. Boyd, Grand Master of Ohio, Prince Hall, who made an attempt to start a Council in that State in the late 1880's. Nothing came of this effort.

On August 14, 1916, the Grand Chapter of Ohio, Prince Hall, set apart and sanctioned the establishment of Councils. Three were authorized: Adonhiram, No. 1, Cleveland; Zabud, No. 2, Toledo; and Herald, No. 3, Columbus. On August 13, 1917 a Convention of delegates from these three Councils organized a Grand Council in Cincinnati, and on December 21, 1920, this body was incorporated. Under its sanction, Councils were established in Dayton, Oberlin, Zanesville, Newark, Portsmouth and Springfield in Ohio; Boston, Massachusetts; Chicago, Illinois; Indianapolis, Indiana; and Pittsburgh, Pennsylvania. The degrees were conferred upon brethren of other jurisdictions and deputies were appointed for Pennsylvania, Indiana, Minnesota, Iowa, Illinois, New York, Rhode Island and Massachusetts. A program was formulated to carry the work into all other Prince Hall jurisdictions. The unsettled conditions of the last ten years have put a check on the work and during this period only one Council was formed (Lima, Ohio). Interest has now been revived and plans to continue the work, as originally planned, are now being considered.

A 36 page printed Transactions of the Grand Council covering the years 1924 and 1925 shows a list of officers and members of twelve of the thirteen Councils (Alpha, No. 6, in Massachusetts having no returns). The total membership then was 465 in the Councils reporting.

Grimshaw described Negro Templarism as deriving from the Duke of Sussex in 1818, by his deputizing Passey Benjamin to establish the Order in the West Indies and North America. He lists the same names in connection with the forming of the Encampments as in the Chapter. This, again, would have made them all at least seventy years of age. St. George Encampment, No. 1, is dated by Grimshaw as being formed on June 12, 1820 in Philadelphia. This is four months before the first Chapter formed, using the Grimshaw dates—which does not seem reasonable.

The next Encampment was Palestine, No. 2, in 1826 and the third, Richmond, No. 3 in 1838. The First African Grand Encampment of North America was formed in 1844, and all Negro Templarism in the United States is derived therefrom.

Of course, we cannot accept such an act of the Duke of Sussex as being historical fact as there are no records of any other such acts on his part in the United States. So, like Negro Capitular Masonry, we shall have to take the date of its commencement in the United States at the forming of the first subordinate Encampment, without knowing "from whence it came."

CHAPTER 14

ANCIENT & ACCEPTED
SCOTTISH RITE

𝒯HE first Supreme Council of the Ancient and Accepted Scottish Rite of the 33rd Degree in the world was founded in Charleston, South Carolina, in 1801. When we realize, after examining the mass of data that has been gathered on the early days of the Rite, how little is known regarding the actual beginning of the system as it is known today, especially where the individuals concerned in its formation received the degrees they had, we cannot expect to find Negro Scottish Rite Masonry having its early history very well defined. There is a claim that a body of the Rite among colored men was formed in Philadelphia, Pennsylvania, some time in 1820 and there is some basis for such a belief. Evidence of some such body appears in a minute book of 1855 in the archives of the Negro Supreme Council in Philadelphia. As there is no further data on the subject we shall pass on to the first definite evidence of the Rite as it exists today among the Negro brethren in the United States.

Grimshaw, in his Chapter on this Rite, is equally as vague as he is on Capitular and Chivalric Masonry. He says that:

"By authority of the Supreme Council of France, and under their direction, Inspector General and Deputy, Dr. St. Larine, of the Supreme Council of France, arrived in the United States in the year 1850 at Philadelphia, Pa., and conferred the Ancient Accepted Scottish Rite degree upon David Leary, a prominent colored Mason in Philadelphia," and that "The Supreme Council of France granted David Leary a patent of power and authority, authorizing and directing him to create inspector generals and establish a Supreme Council of the Ancient Accepted Rite among the colored Masons in the United States of America."

NEGRO MASONRY IN THE UNITED STATES

By "Dr. St. Larine" is undoubtedly meant de Jachim De Santa Rosa De Roune De St. Laurent, Marquis De Santa Rosa, Count De St. Laurent, former Captain and Commodore of the Mexican Navy, etc., etc.

Robert Folger, Cerneau Scottish Rite historian, says Laurent came to New York City in 1832 and "took upon himself the title of Most Puissant Grand Commander, ad vitam, of the Supreme Grand Council of the Thirty-third degree, Supreme Chief of the Ancient and Modern Free Masonry, for Newfoundland, North America, Mexico on both seas, the Canary Islands, etc." With Elias Hicks of the old Cerneau Scottish Rite body, he formed the "Hicks-St. Laurent Council" under the title "United Supreme Council of the Western Hemisphere" which fell to pieces after about two years, when St. Laurent returned to France.

We have little knowledge of the travels and activities of St. Laurent after he returned to France in 1834, if, indeed, we have much knowledge of him at all. There is, however, ample evidence extant to base a conclusion that he did confer degrees on Negro Freemasons.

From information now at hand, as recorded in a minute book of the body, "A Supreme Grand Council of S.∴I.∴G.∴of the thirty third degree of the A∴ and A∴ Rite, was held in Philadelphia city" on December 10, 1854. Another was held on December 22. In February, 1855, the next was held and then followed meetings on April 8, April 14 and September 2nd.

On January 6, 1856 "A Supreme Grand Council of M.P.S.G.I. General of the A. and A. Scottish Rite was held at the Council Chamber," with David Leary, M.P.S.G.C., presiding and four others, designated as D.D.C.; Lieut. G.C.; C. of G.; and M. of C. Due to vacancies it was found necessary to "exhalt four S.P.R.S. to the 33d°." Ballot was taken and four brethren were selected. "Bodies of the 31st and 32nd° were then opened" and one of those elected who had not received these two degrees was advanced and then all four were crowned 33rd degree Masons. "The M.P.G.C. presented a copy of the Secret Constitutions which were read for the enlightenment of the Council." Then we find the following in the minutes:

"There exists no legally formed body of this Rite among Masons of Color and as the right is guaranteed to all Inspectors General by the Secret Constitutions to open Lodges of Perfection, hold Councils of Kts. of E. and P. of J. and to confer in Chapter of such the degrees of Kts. R. De H.R.D.M., Councils of the E. and W. and all other degrees acknowledged by this particular Rite and whereas the M.P.S.G.C. by Patent emanating from the Grand Orient of France has been created and clothed with powers, dignity and authority of Sov. G. I. G., and also invested with authority to name and install his associates as he shall choose so to do from time to time. And as in the exercise of that power he has created a lawful number of Inspectors which are now assembled in open Council, Therefore, Be it Known that a Supreme Grand Council of the 33rd and last degree of Masonry according to the Ancient and Accepted Scottish Rite is hereby established and in accordance with the Secret Consitutions the said Council claims exclusive jurisdiction in the United States of North America over all bodies of Colored Masons practicing the sublime degrees to the 33rd and last," etc., etc.

Then appears a record of other business in the minutes and also a listing of the nine brethren and their titles of office with the Statutes and Regulations.

About 1864, Baron A. Hugo de Bulow, 33°, a member of the Grand Orient of France, conferred the Scottish Rite Degrees on four brethren and created them Deputy Inspectors General, 33°, as follows:

Dr. Peter W. Ray   for New York
Jonathan Miller   for Pennsylvania
Levi Anderson   for Delaware
Lemuel G. Griffin   for Maryland

These brethren were members of lodges subordinate to Grand Lodges recognized by the National Compact Grand Lodge. The Supreme Council formed in Philadelphia in 1856 by David Leary, drew its membership from brethren not allied with the National Compact bodies. Dr. Ray formed a Supreme Council for North America and its Dependencies, with headquarters in New York, this body drawing its candidates from the Compact Grand Lodge subordinates.

The Southern members of the Rite did not believe that such a large territory should be covered by a single Supreme Council and, thereupon, Lemuel G. Griffin, 33°, established a Supreme Council for the Southern Jurisdiction, with headquarters in Baltimore, Maryland. The year previous the Leary Supreme Council in Philadelphia authorized the establishment of a fourth Supreme Council in Washington, D.C., for the Southern and Western Jurisdiction, for Independent Masons. In 1871, Joshua D. Kelley, who had received his 33° at the hands of Griffin in Baltimore, with six others, established a fifth Supreme Council at Philadelphia for Independent Masons—called King Frederick Supreme Council.

Thus by 1872, five Negro Supreme Councils were in active existence in the United States, as follows:

Formed	Name	Place	Founder
1—1856—Northern Jurisdiction		Philadelphia	David Leary
2—1864—United States		New York	Peter W. Ray
3—1869—Southern and Western		Washington	T. A. Jackson
4—1870—Southern Jurisdiction		Baltimore	Lemuel G. Griffin
5—1871—King Frederick		Philadelphia	Joshua D. Kelley

The Supreme Councils numbered 1, 3 and 5 were Independent bodies, the others were National Compact.

On April 1, 1880 the New York body issued a call for representatives of all of the Supreme Councils to meet in New York on June 3, 1880 "to deliberate and devise for the better establishment of the Ancient and Accepted Scottish Rite among Colored men in this country." The meeting actually took place on October 21st, but no definite action resulted excepting the passage of a Resolution to convene the representatives again on January 13, 1881. On this date eighteen Inspectors General convened in Corinthian Hall, New York City, as follows; four from No. 1; five from No. 2; one from No. 3; four from No. 4; and four from No. 5. John S. Chase and Samuel R. Scottron of the New York body were elected Chairman and Secretary, respectively. The result was an agreement to form two Supreme Councils—one to be called the Northern and the other the Southern Jurisdiction. The first to have twenty-nine States and Alaska and the other eighteen States and two Territories. Among various arrangements for the reorganization was the plan for the two Philadelphia and the New York Councils to have five representatives each selected to convene and elect officers; the Washington and Baltimore to have seven each for the Southern Jurisdiction. Also the Baron Bulow "work" was adopted for both jurisdictions.

In the latter part of February, 1881, the two Philadelphia Supreme Councils made arrangements for the Convention to elect officers in the Northern Jurisdiction but no delegates from the New York Supreme Council appeared on the date selected for the meeting. Those present retired and notified Dr. Ray that they would again convene on April 8th. In the meantime, the two Philadelphia bodies held separate meetings and selected two additional representatives each, so that, in case the New York delegates failed to attend again, they could legally convene. At ten o'clock in the morning of the date selected, the representatives met in Liberty Hall, 718 Lombard St., Philadelphia. Late in the afternoon, without any delegates or any word from the New York Supreme Council, they proceeded to organize a Convention with sixteen delegates present. A permanent organization was then effected with Moses Wheeler of the King Frederick Supreme Council as Chairman. They then adjourned.

On the following date they elected William Cooper of King Darius Supreme Council as Sovereign Grand Commander, and a full set of officers. Under the name of the "United Supreme Council, 33°, for the Northern Jurisdiction of the United States," they adopted a Constitution; Deputies were appointed for Iowa, Massachusetts, Minnesota, Missouri, New Jersey, New York and Ohio. The roll of Inspectors at the organization shows forty-seven names. In 1908 there were fifty names. In 1926 the membership of the Rite was 5,210 Sovereign Princes.

On January 27, 1887, in Washington, D. C., the two bodies of the Southern Jurisdiction formed the "United Supreme Council, 33°, A.A.S. Rite for the Southern Jurisdiction of the United States of America." They elected James A. Handy, 33°, of the Washington Supreme Council as Sovereign Grand Commander, and a set of officers. In 1907 their roll showed one hundred and fifty names as Inspectors. In 1924 this jurisdiction published a set of abridged rituals of the 4th to 32nd degree.

The Northern Supreme Council has a very fine cathedral in Philadelphia. The movement to erect the building started in 1921 and on October 16, 1927 the ground was broken. On May 12, 1928 the structure was dedicated being completely finished and equipped. From a listing of the present Consistories under its control we find forty-three in sixteen States. They are numbered, the last being sixty-five, so that it would appear that twenty-two have become dormant.

The United Supreme Council was originally incorporated under the laws of New Jersey with a name exactly like that of the white Supreme Council. In 1924 the latter Supreme Council negotiated with the Negro Supreme Council (the two Sovereign Grand Commanders meeting in person) with the result that the words "Prince Hall Affiliation" were added to the name of the Colored Supreme Council. A news release, dated Boston, Massachusetts, September 22, 1924, announced the fact and the Transactions of the Northern Supreme Council (white) on page 37 (1924) refer to the matter in which the late Leon S. Abbott, Grand Commander, said:

"I feel that the whole matter was finally disposed of in a way that cannot embarrass us in the future, and at the same time, in a way satisfactory to our colored friends."

The Southern Jurisdiction likewise has a Cathedral in Washington, D. C., of ample proportions. Both buildings are well kept and a credit to Freemasonry in our country. They also have libraries containing rare items of Negro Masonry, Proceedings, etc.

Beyond and in contradistinction, considering the above, there is another colored Scottish Rite body in the United States, whose lineage and history has not been, until recently, very clear—and even now no attempt will be made to do more than quote from a "100 Anniversary" program of twenty-eight pages, published for this Anniversary. The affair was held in "Masonic Temple, 315 South Rampart Street, New Orleans, Louisiana, on Friday, October 27th, 1939."

On page eight we find a historical digest of the establishment of "a Sovereign Grand Consistory of Supreme Chiefs of Exalted Masonry on August 28, 1807" by Joseph Cerneau, who, says the account, "arrived at New York from Cuba in August 1806." One of these dates must be corrected—the "Sovereign Grand Consistory" had its inception on October 28, 1807 and was not completed until October, 1808.

A footnote in the Louisiana program advises that "Cerneau received his authority from Etienne (Stephen) Morin." Again this is an error for Cerneau was simply appointed a Deputy Inspector General of the Rite of Perfection by Antoine du Potet, for the Northern part of the Island of Cuba, with power to initiate Master Masons from the Fourth to the Twenty-fourth Degrees, provided that these Masons had been officers of a Lodge, regularly constituted; and with further power to confer the Twenty-fifth Degree on but one Knight Prince Mason each year.

Cerneau later went beyond his authority by operating in New York City so that any and all the bodies which were set up by him directly or indirectly, were irregularly constituted. But what is more to the point, they were bodies of the Rite of Perfection only and not Scottish Rite bodies, altho the degrees he propagated were, in part, used to make up the Scottish Rite also. That the Cerneau bodies later added other degrees to the system and changed their name to that of Scottish Rite, does not alter the situation in the least.

To continue with extracts from the pamphlet, "On the 17th of October, 1839, the M. Ill. B. Santangelo (Orzio de Attellis, Marquis de Santangelo, created a 33rd. In the valley of New York, on the 16th of November, 1827, by M. Ill. B. Joseph Cerneau), Roca de Sante Pietri (Jose Antonion Roca de Sante Pietri, created a 33rd on the 10th of April, 1832, by the National Supreme Council of Spain), J. J. Conte (created a 33rd, by the Supreme Council of the Grand Orient of France on the 20th of May, 1822). F. Burtheau, and R. E. de David-Perdreauville, all Sovereign Grand Inspectors General, held a meeting and organized a Supreme Council for the United States of America. The reason for which they took this title is found in the fact that the United Supreme Council for the Western Hemisphere, which in 1836 existed in the City of New York, under the Grand Commandership of T. M. Ill. B. Elias Hicks, was then slumbering, and there was no recognized authority for the Scotch [sic] Rite in the United States."

"This Supreme Council for the United States of America became the Supreme Council of Louisiana by an act of incorporation March 16, 1870, granted at an extra session of the legislature of Louisiana."

In a list of the "Grand Officers of the Supreme Council— 1859" we find "Most Powerful Sovereign Grand Commander, Ill. B. James Foulhouze," the mere mention of whom will be significant to Masonic scholars.

On page twenty and twenty-one is a list of "Some of the Sovereign Grand Inspectors General created 33rd Masons by the Supreme Council of Louisiana," with dates. There are one hundred and sixty names, starting with Jean Lamother, September 27, 1845 and ending with five created on November 27, 1936. It is noted that George Longe, the present Most Powerful Sovereign Grand Commander, is listed under the date of November 30, 1925, with two others for the same date, one being the present "Powerful Grand Treasurer." They were the first created after a lapse of thirteen years.

There is also a list of Grand Commanders from de Santangelo (October 27, 1839) down to George Longe (July 21, 1939). It contains eighteen names, six of whom served two terms with others in between. Only three terms were ten years or more (10, 11 and 21 years).

Further historical review and external data are not necessary to bring out the lineage of this body. What has been quoted above and the remarks thereon will preclude the necessity of going further into matters already too well known to Masonic historians of the Scottish Rite. The body is an outgrowth of the Cerneau Rite of Perfection group in New York City, which finally became colored

ORIGIN AND OBJECTS

OF

ANCIENT FREEMASONRY;

ITS

INTRODUCTION INTO THE UNITED STATES,

AND

LEGITIMACY AMONG COLORED MEN.

A TREATISE DELIVERED BEFORE

St. Cyprian Lodge, No 13, June 24th, A. D. 1853----A. L. 5853.

BY

M. R. DELANY, K. M., D. D. G. H P.

"Great is Truth, and must prevail"

PITTSBURGH:

PRINTED BY W S HAVEN, CORNER MARKET AND SECOND STREETS

1853.

Title Page of earliest printed work
on Negro Freemasonry

following visits to their lodges in 1867 by Oscar J. Dunn, Grand Master of Prince Hall Masons in Louisiana, and others from various Negro lodges.

Statistics of membership of the number of bodies now operating are wanting. In the Celebration program eighteen Lodges; three Rose Croix Chapters; one Council of Kadosh and the Grand Consistory and Supreme Council are listed as taking part. Also eleven Eastern Star Chapters and The Martha Grand Chapter, a body created on December 29, 1929. An additional list of "some Lodges chartered by the Supreme Council" shows fifty-three. Lists of Rose Croix Chapters, seventeen, and Councils of Kadosh, fourteen. There seems to be only one Consistory, however, some data concerning it being as follows:

"On June 19, 1813, several brethren in New Orleans petitioned the Supreme Council of Sovereign Grand Inspectors General of the 33rd degree, for the United States," etc., "for a Council of Princes of the Royal Secret, 32nd degree." It further states that the petition was granted and "Ill. Brethren Joseph Cerneau, De Witt Clinton, and James N. Durand were elected Honorary Members."

While no information is at hand to confirm any opinion, this body probably is not in fraternal amity with the other two Negro Supreme Councils in the United States. At least, members of the Northern Jurisdiction have little knowledge of the Louisiana group.

CHAPTER 15

THE EASTERN STAR
AMONG COLORED PEOPLE

*T*HE date of the earliest Eastern Star Chapter established by colored people is not known. During the early days of the propagation of the Rite, rituals could be purchased with ease. No doubt Chapters were formed without the formality of a charter by colored persons who had come by the degrees by way of these rituals.

The first colored Grand Chapter of the Eastern Star was formed only about ten years after the establishment of the first Grand Chapter in the world. It is the Supreme Grand Chapter, O.E.S., for North Carolina, established at Washington, in that state, in September, 1880. There are thirty-seven Grand Chapters now functioning, but in some states, such as Washington, Missouri, Louisiana and West Virginia, there are two Grand Chapters.

As an indication of the membership, statistics for 1925 show 3,434 Chapters having 121,101 members. The economic conditions of recent years, however, had a very great effect on the membership in these groups. Original Eureka Grand Chapter of New York had 41 Chapters with 2,231 members in 1924 while in 1936 it had 39 Chapters with only 940 members.

In 1907 a "Supreme Grand Chapter, Order of the Eastern Star," was formed in Boston, Massachusetts, but at its Third Session, held in Detroit, Michigan, on August 23-25, 1910, the name was changed to "Inter-state Conference of Grand Chapters of the Order of the Eastern Star."

The organization meeting held in 1907 was called by Mrs. Letitia L. Foy of Massachusetts. The officers elected were:

Kittie Terrell (Illinois Juris.)	Supreme Grand Royal Matron
Walden Banks (Mass. & R. I. Juris.)	Supreme Grand Royal Patron
Viola Hart (Georgia Juris.)	Associate Grand Royal Matron
Addie Duffin (Maryland Juris.)	Grand Royal Treasurer

The biennial meetings have been held as follows:

2—Chicago, Ill.   Aug. 21-22, 1908   15 Grand Juris. Rep.
3—Detroit, Mich.   Aug. 23-25, 1910   12 Grand Juris. Rep.
4—Washington, D. C.,   Aug. 21-22, 1912   11 Grand Juris. Rep.
5—Pittsburgh, Pa.   Aug. 4 - 6, 1914 12 States Rep.
6—Chicago, Ill.   Aug. 23-26, 1916   18 States Rep.
7—Kansas City, Mo.   (called off because of the War)
8—Cincinnati, Ohio   Aug. 23-26, 1920   20 States Rep.
9—Washington, D.C.   Aug. 7-10, 1922   21 States Rep.
10—Pittsburg, Pa.   Aug. 19-22, 1924   32 States Rep.

Previous to 1920 the Inter-state Conference adopted a resolution incorporating the Order of the Amaranth into the Eastern Star but in 1922, it was withdrawn into a separate organization.

The Grand Chapters have adopted distinctive titles, more or less following a like system in Grand Lodges of colored Freemasonry, such as Eureka, Prince Hall, Excelsior, Queen Bathsheba, etc.

The Golden State Grand Chapter, O.E.S., in California has a "Youth's Fraternity" as does the Amaranthus Grand Chapter, O.E.S. of Nebraska.

The Grand Chapter, O.E.S. of Virginia, having about 5,000 members, owns property valued over $50,000, and has an Endowment Insurance Department. In Illinois, Georgia and Indiana the bodies have combined with the Masonic bodies in running or owning Homes for the aged.

NAMES OF GRAND CHAPTERS, O.E.S.

Supreme Grand Chapter of North Carolina, organized in September, 1880.

Excelsior Grand Chapter of Tennessee, organized, June, 1881.

Golden State Grand Chapter of California, organized in December, 1882.

Prince Hall Grand Chapter of Kansas, organized in August, 1883.

Eureka Grand Chapter of Louisiana, organized June 30, 1884.

Grand Chapter of Kentucky, organized in August, 1885.

Grand Chapter of Arkansas, organized July 12, 1886.

Grand Chapter of Ohio, organized August 3, 1887.

Indiana Grand Chapter, organized October 25, 1888.

Wolverine Grand Chapter of Michigan, organized August 21, 1889.

Masonic Grand Chapter of Texas, organized January 20, 1890.

Eureka Grand Chapter of Illinois, organized August 11, 1890.

District of Columbia Grand Chapter, organized May 24, 1892.

Grand Chapter of Ontario, Canada, organized in April, 1894.

Mizpah Grand Chapter of Alabama, organized June 21, 1894.

Prince Hall Grand Chapter of New England, organized November 3, 1894.

Bathsheba Grand Chapter of Mississippi, organized during 1894 (date unknown).

Original Eureka Grand Chapter of New York, organized October 18, 1895.

Maryland Grand Chapter, organized in November, 1896 (Grand Chapter of Maryland).

Grand Chapter of Georgia, organized June 3, 1898.

Queen Bathsheba Grand Chapter of Oklahoma, organized August 9, 1898.

Masonic Grand Chapter of Virginia, organized July 26, 1903.

Electa Grand Chapter of Iowa, organized May 21, 1907.

Grand Chapter of South Carolina, organized July 10, 1908.

Deborah Grand Chapter of Pennsylvania, organized in November, 1909.

Oziel Grand Chapter of New Jersey, organized June 24, 1913.

Electa Grand Chapter of West Virginia, organized in June, 1913.

Prince Hall Grand Chapter of West Virginia, organized July 16, 1914.

Grand Chapter of Arizona, organized July 11, 1921.

Amaranthus Grand Chapter of Nebraska, organized October 15, 1921.

Columbine Grand Chapter of Colorado, organized July 24, 1922.

Esther Grand Chapter of Louisiana, organized January 12, 1938.

Bethlehem Grand Chapter of Florida (date unknown).

Grand Chapter of Delaware (date unkown).

Grand Chapter of Minnesota (date unknown).

There are two bodies in the State of Washington one of which was formed in July, 1913. The names are: Mount Tacoma Grand Chapter and the United Grand Chapter.

Also two in Missouri one of which was formed in December, 1890. The names are: United Grand Chapter and the Harmony Grand Chapter.

The General Grand Chapter of the Continent of Africa was organized at Monrovia, Liberia, January 24, 1903.

HEROINES OF JERICHO AND OTHER ALLIED GROUPS

The Heroines of Jericho Degree is accredited to David Vinton, one of the Masonic Lecturers of the early nineteenth century. The earliest form of the degree in print is that of William Leigh, P.G.M. of Alabama (white) in his book "Ladies Masonry," 1851.

In 1866, G. W. Brown, in Michigan, included this degree with the "Mason's Daughter" and "Kindred" degrees, in a ritual which he published.

From what source the Negro brethren obtained the degree is not known, unless it was from one or both of the above books. The present ritual "Court of Heroines of Jericho by Moses Dickson, Grand Venerable of All Courts and Past Grand Master of Masons" (Negro) entered in the office of the Librarian of Congress in 1895, was printed and sold by The Moses Dickson Regalia and Supply Co., Kansas City, Missouri. It contains the "Master Mason's Daughter;" the "True Kinsman," and "Heroines of Jericho" degrees. It is a small book of seventy-two pages.

Moses Dickson was made a Prince Hall Mason under Ohio jurisdiction and at the formation of the Grand Lodge of Missouri (Negro) in 1866 was made Grand Lecturer. He became second Grand Master in 1868 and also served in that capacity in 1877. Out of twenty-five meetings of his Grand Lodge, he is listed as being present at fifteen including August 16, 1898. No doubt he was present at others. Dickson Lodge, No. 11 (Prince Hall) of Lexington, Missouri, was named after him.

Until recently very little was known of any earlier activity of a body of the Heroines of Jericho. Now a "Constitution and General Regulations for the Government of Courts of the Adoptive Rite or

Female Masonry," Philadelphia, Pa., 1872, has come to light, together with two printed rituals of the same date, covering these same three degrees. They are in the library of the United Supreme Council, A.A.S.R. (Prince Hall), Northern Jurisdiction, in Philadelphia.

The title of the general head of the body was then known as the Grand General Superintendent of Courts. The Heroines of Jericho degree could only be given to Royal Arch Masons, their wives and widows, altho the other two degrees could be conferred on Master Masons, their wives, widows, unmarried sisters and daughters over sixteen years of age. These qualifications are not to be found in the Dickson requirements, where Master Masons, etc., are eligible to all three degrees, just as they are in the present organization of like nature organized by white sisters and brothers in San Francisco, California on June 29, 1894 and reorganized in Chicago, Illinois on December 15, 1905.

In a minute book, which records a single meeting of the Grand Encampment, K.T. (Negro) for December 27, 1867, held at Philadelphia are a number of copies of certificates issued by Jonathan Davis, M.D., Grand General Superintendent of Courts, as follows:

1—Nov. 1, 1872—Illinois—William Lyman Darrow.

2—Nov. 13, 1872—Pennsylvania—Robert W. Bell.

3—June 7, 1873—Southern Carolina—Richard Howell Gleaves.

4—Sept. 1, 1873—New York—Enos A. Hall.

5—Feb. 20, 1874—Tennessee—Samuel W. Ware.

There are also two charters recorded:

1—Naoma Court, No. 2, Pittsburg, Pa.—Nov. 12, 1872

2—Mary's Court, No. 3—Philadelphia, Pa.—Mar. 28, 1872

They both state that the year of issue (1872) is the twenty-fifth year of the Order, which would take it back to 1847, the year that Rob Morris, originator of the Eastern Star degrees, received the Heroines of Jericho degree himself.

Another interesting certificate, a copy of which is in the book, is that issued to "Sister Catherine E. Hall, wife of Companion Enos A. Hall," dated Nov. 2, 1872, certifying her receipts of the degrees.

At the present time there are sixteen Grand Courts of the Order, operating in 21 states and the District of Columbia, some of which support homes and other charities.

Other "allied" bodies exist among the Negro brethren. The Daughters of Isis is one which is conferred on ladies. Little is known of the formation of the bodies which confer the degrees, nor of its archives. It is active in Ohio and possibly a few other States. It is an auxiliary to the "Shrine."

FOREWORD TO PART TWO

This Part is devoted to "recognized" Negro Freemasonry. Aside from the first and last Chapters, it is the history of a single lodge. It is unique because it is the only one in the United States operating under the ægis of a white Grand Lodge, which is composed wholly of Negroes, or has more than a single Negro in it.

Grimshaw devoted a page and a half to this lodge in his book, but practically all of the account is in error. In Clark's "The Negro Mason in Equity" which is one of the finest brochures on Negro Masonry ever written, the page about the lodge is likewise incorrect. It is unfortunate not to have, in this otherwise excellent work, this material which could easily have been presented as ably as the other data in the pamphlet. The conclusion is particularly misleading, "the lodge was finally allowed to die, and the colored brethren made therein set adrift without chart or compass." Just why the Negro historians have been unable to present a story of the lodge based on fact is not easy to explain because the main features are in the Proceedings of the Grand Lodge of New Jersey (white), and the volumes easily accessible. But these inaccuracies are not confined to Negro historians, for some of the most ridiculous articles in the general literature of the Craft are about this lodge. The printed articles are not nearly as queer as some of the oral "information" imparted to "uninformed brethren." Two of the points of confusion are the origin of the lodge and its present status. The latter is usually stated to be that the Grand Lodge of New Jersey has prohibited further initiations of Negroes so that, when all the members die, it will pass out of existence. I mention this in particular because this very statement is what originally brought my attention to the lodge in 1920. An examination of the Proceedings of the Grand Lodge of New Jersey at that time showed that sixty-one Master Masons had been made in the lodge in the twenty years previous. This didn't look like a "waiting to die" proposition to me.

What now follows in this Part must not be confused with Negro Freemasonry as covered in Part I. This is simply the history of a subordinate lodge of the Grand Lodge of New Jersey (white) which was chartered as a lodge composed of white brethren, who initiated some Negroes and, finally, after about fifty years, became wholly composed of Negroes.

PART II

RECOGNIZED NEGRO FREEMASONRY

CHAPTER 1

NEGRO MASONS IN WHITE LODGES BEFORE 1870

ON June 24, 1848, a Grand Lodge of Negro Masons was organized in Trenton, New Jersey. It received no notice from the sixty-one year old white Grand Lodge which had been formed at New Brunswick, New Jersey, on January 30, 1787.

This was not the first Grand Lodge of Negro Masons in the United States. In fact it was the fifth, the others being Massachusetts, June 24, 1791; Pennsylvania, December 27, 1815; New York, March 14, 1845; and the District of Columbia, March 27, 1848. None of these Grand Lodges was "recognized" by the white Grand Lodges. Nevertheless, even prior to the Civil War, references to Colored Freemasons in regular white lodges are to be found in the literature of the Craft. Such items as the following are examples:

PROCEEDINGS OF TEMPLE LODGE, No. 11, of Delaware, by Andrew E. Sanborn, P.M., 1917, page 109.

"*Negro Visitor*—It is also interesting to note that among the visitors on the evening of October 9, 1850, was a negro, one Jehu Jones, of Acadia Lodge, No. 345, Dartmont, Nova Scotia."

Acadia Lodge, No. 345, on the Register of the Grand Lodge of Scotland, was organized at Dartmouth (not Dartmont) during the Provincial Grand Mastership of the Hon. J. Leander Starr (appointed in 1844 by the Grand Master of Scotland). In 1851, Athol Lodge No. 361, on the same Register, was established as an offshoot of Acadia Lodge, No. 345, and soon afterward No. 345 returned its warrant.

HISTORY AND MASONIC RECORD OF NEWARK LODGE, No. 7, of Newark, New Jersey by J. Edward Blackmore, P.M., 1927, page 48:

" 'John Williams, a colored man, having been announced as a visitor, was, after examination, admitted.' "

This minute is dated September 4, 1838 and the meeting was held in St. John's Hall, in Newark, the Lodge being then numbered 55. In commenting on this record W.·.Brother Blackmore says:

"The fact that a special mention of his visitation was made in the body of the minutes, indicates that it was, at least, an unusual occurrence and it is quite probable that he was the first colored Mason who ever visited the Lodge."

A CENTENNIAL HISTORY OF MORNING STAR LODGE, 1793-1893, of Worcester, Massachusetts, by Edward S. Nason, 1894, page 220. The author tells of Fraternal Army Lodge, No. 4, in the Civil War, sponsored by Morning Star Lodge, and how this Army lodge held its communications in New Bern, North Carolina, in which was located St. John's Lodge, No. 3. The lodge was located in a fine hall of which he says:

"This property was owned by St. John's Lodge, and near by lived a black man who had been made a Mason and a member of the Lodge that he might be Tyler."

This Lodge was in the 25th Massachusetts Volunteer Militia and was warranted on October 17, 1861 by William D. Coolidge, Grand Master of Massachusetts. Its first meeting was held in Annapolis, Maryland, on December 23, 1861 and its last on March 28, 1865 in New Bern—in all forty-six communications were held.

The Proceedings of the Grand Lodge of North Carolina show Brother William H. Hancock (sometimes spelled Handcock), to whom this item refers, as Tyler of the lodge for 1849, 50, 51 and 52, and as a member for several years afterward. About the time of the Civil War he moved to Cleveland, Ohio, according to an account of him in a magazine article.

Brother Hancock petitioned St. John's Lodge on April 8, 1846. He was initiated April 13, passed May 7 and raised on June 1, 1846. The present Secretary of the Lodge states that he was "a very attentive member" and confirms his Tylership of four years. As the Lodge has no records from 1853 to the Civil War, it is not known when or how he severed his membership in the lodge.

The earliest record of a Negro actually being a member of a white lodge in the United States is found in 1844, but from evidence extant, it is obvious that the brethren involved were made Free-masons at a much earlier date. In fact, so far as one of them is concerned, a membership as early as 1821 can be shown. (See Appendix).

These instances of Negroes being Freemasons in white lodges are by no means all that could be cited but they will show that what is to follow cannot be considered the first time that Negroes were admitted into white lodges. The Civil War brought prominence to the Negro question and a hope that, along with emancipation, would come a more liberal attitude upon the part of Freemasonry also. On the contrary, in some Masonic jurisdictions legislation of a prohibitive nature was passed upon the admitting of Negroes to the Fraternity. For years Negro lodges had asked for recognition but now renewed efforts in this direction were made in several jurisdictions. The general attitude of the Craft, as a whole, however, was to look upon Freemasonry as a province of white men.

In New Jersey quite a number of the Abolitionists who were Freemasons were more inclined to look with favor upon the question of Negro Masons. One of the more prominent of these was M∴W∴ William Silas Whitehead, Grand Master of New Jersey 1864 to 1867, inclusive. In his Annual Address to Grand Lodge, as he retired from office, he voiced his belief in the practical application of the "universal brotherhood of man," specifically stating that he included men of all colors and religious affiliations. He was especially commended by the Committee on Grand Master's Address.

There seems little doubt that the address of Grand Master White-head eventually came into the hands of some of the unrecognized Negro Masons—possibly they had it called to their attention. In any event, a short time afterward that which constitutes the historical review to follow began to transpire, culminating in the establishment of a lodge in New Jersey, which eventually became Negro and which, being one of the subordinate lodges of the white Grand Lodge of New Jersey, is a "recognized" Lodge.

77

CHAPTER 2

FIRST PETITION OF NEGROES TO GRAND LODGE

*T*HE 83rd Annual Communication of the Grand Lodge of New Jersey was held in Taylor Opera House, Trenton, New Jersey, on January 19 and 20, 1870. The Grand Master, M∴W∴Henry R. Cannon, in his address to Grand Lodge, included these words:

"The attention of the Grand Lodge is called to an application of Colored Masons for recognition and connection with this Grand Lodge, to be presented at the present session. I solicit in their behalf, a respectful consideration of their petition, and careful inquiry as to the claims they may present for reception, within the bounds of our Ancient Fraternity."

The Committee on Grand Master's address referred this to the Committee on Jurisprudence and Charity. The Committee reported as follows:

"The petition of Colored persons, claiming to be Masons, praying recognition by this Grand Lodge, and inquiring as to the proper steps to be taken by them to bring themselves within the jurisdiction of this Grand Lodge, is couched in respectful language, and is entitled to courteous consideration. The questions which arise in connection with this petition are of great and increasing importance, and require a more careful and studious investigation than your committee can give to them at the present communication. It is therefore recommended that a Special Committee be appointed, to have an interview with the parties in charge of the petition, to consider questions therein, and to report at the next Annual Communication of this Grand Lodge."

This report was adopted and the following brethren composed the Committee:

P.G.M. Joseph Trimble, No. 15
P.G.M. William Silas Whitehead, No. 1
P.M. Rev. Henry Veshlage, Jr., No. 10

Immediately following this piece of business, the Committee on Dispensations and Warrants reported:

"The petition of John L. H. Severs, [sic] Jeremiah Evans and others, for a warrant for a Lodge to be called Cushite Lodge, to be located in Newark, is not in due form and is not accompanied by the recommendation of any neighboring Lodge, as required by the General Regulations.

"For these and other reasons satisfactory to your committee, they report the same back with a recommendation that the prayer of the petitioners be not granted."

The reasons cited were violations of the Sixth Section of the By-Laws and the Second and Third Sections of the General Regulations of the Grand Lodge.

It will be noted that the Lodge was to be called "Cushite Lodge." Cush was the eldest son of Ham. The use of the term "Cushite" is external evidence that the persons involved were colored men for Cush is a Biblical name for Ethiopia.

Just what lodge or lodges the petitioners held membership in is not known. The earliest known Negro Lodge in Newark is David's Independent Lodge, No. 2, warranted on April 23, 1842. At a much later date—and probably after the dormancy of the above lodge, two other lodges were chartered, Prudence, No. 26 and Bethany, No. 31. It is probable that they were members of one of these lodges.

At the next Annual Communication of Grand Lodge, the Special Committee reported upon the matter entrusted to their care. They reiterated what had been said in the report of the Committee on Warrants and Dispensations at the previous Annual Communication and, in addition, added some information purporting to be accepted as the derivation of "Prince Hall" or Colored Masonry in the United States. This included a copy of the Charter issued to Prince Hall by the Grand Lodge of England (Moderns) on September 29, 1784. The final paragraphs of the report read:

"Your Committee do therefore recommend that the petition and the accompanying document be returned to the petitioners together with a copy of this report.

"Your Committee, in conclusion, deem it consistent with the duty assigned to them, to intimate to the petitioners that there is one, and but one, regular way in which their purpose of affiliation with this Grand Lodge can be realized, and that is, by pursuing the same process to which all profanes are subjected. The doors of the Masonic Lodges of New Jersey are open to all men freeborn and of lawful age, of every clime, of every color, of every creed, who declare their trust to be in God, have passed the scrutiny of a Committee of a lawful Lodge, and have achieved the favorable verdict of the secret ballot."

Thus closed the "Cushite Lodge" incident.

CHAPTER 3

ALPHA LODGE IS CHARTERED

*T*HAT which has been recorded in the previous Chapter has concerned matters in which colored men have been involved. We now come to that which concerns the beginning of Alpha Lodge, in which only white brethren are involved .

It must be brought to mind that the period in which the formation of this lodge took place was just after the Civil War. The Thirteenth Amendment to the Constitution of the United States had been certified by the Secretary of State on December 18, 1865; the Fourteenth Amendment on July 28, 1868; and the Fifteenth Amendment on March 30, 1870. On this last date five States held elections. In New Jersey two Negroes made use of their new voting privilege. Tom Peterson (Munday) voted fifteen minutes after the polls opened at Perth Amboy and another Negro voted in Princeton late in the afternoon. On January 31, 1872, the day the new lodge held its first regular Communication, in the New Jersey Senate a Negro Methodist Minister (Appendix XIV—Woodlin) opened the Legislature with prayer. The attitude of the public toward colored people had taken a decided change yet the Masonic events which so quickly followed, while in line with the trend of the movements then afoot, seem strange in the light of the slow moving and slow changing body of the Craft.

It must be remembered, too, that all organizations which have an existence of years, are builded around a set of ideals. In striving to live up to their ideals do surviving organizations owe their existence. Organizations being made up of human beings, ideals are rarely consummated, however.

Freemasonry, like and among other worthwhile and long existing organizations, has ideals—among which are that no one shall be excluded from membership because of color, race or creed. While there are, as has been shown, isolated cases of Negroes becoming members of white lodges prior to this time, they are exceptional occurrences. A single Masonic brother, aided by a mere handful of others, who believed in putting these particular ideals into practice, is primarily responsible for the introduction of colored men into regular white Masonry. It was he who presented the "Cushite Lodge" petition to the Grand Lodge of New Jersey in 1870, which, having been thwarted, he resolved to accomplish by another method, the nature of which will soon become apparent.

On December 27, 1870, Brother Israel Baldwin, P.M., Nathan Mingus, and William M. Clarke, all of St. John's Lodge, No. 1, of Newark, Brother George E. P. Howard, holding a demit from Eureka Lodge, No. 39, also of Newark, and Brother Herman P. Witzel, holding a demit from Kilwinning Lodge, No. 311, Chicago, Illinois, met in Brother Baldwin's office at 262 Plane Street, Newark, to discuss a proposition for the formation of a new Lodge in Newark.

On December 30th, they met again at the same place and decided to form a Lodge, which Brother Howard suggested be named "Alpha" meaning "One" or "the First," the name being the first letter of the Greek Alphabet. Brother Howard was appointed a Committee to secure a lodge room. They then adjourned to meet on January 14, 1871, at St. John's Lodge, No. 1, when these three members of the Lodge, plus Brothers Marcus W. Adams and Samuel Morrow, Jr., of the same Lodge, applied for and received demits, after advising the Lodge that they expected to apply to Grand Lodge for a Warrant for a new Lodge to be situated in Newark. They requested St. John's Lodge to recommend them at the Grand Lodge Communication to be held that same month, and the Lodge agreed to the request. On January 14th, they held another meeting at which time Brother Howard, who had been appointed for the purpose, together with Brothers Howells and Adams, presented a design for the Lodge seal which was adopted.

Brother Rusling was M.'.W.'.Grand Master of the Grand Lodge of New Jersey for 1870. In his Annual Address on January 18, 1871, among other recommendations for warrants, he said:

"I received also one from nine brethren, accompanied by the recommendation of St. John's Lodge, No. 1, for the formation of a New Lodge in the city of Newark, to be hailed as Alpha Lodge. I know no reason why warrants should not be issued for these Lodges."

The Committee on Warrants reported on January 19, 1871, "that warrant be granted . . . to Alpha Lodge, in the City of Newark, with the officers named in the petition, as No. 116."

Alpha Lodge, No. 116, was constituted in St. John's Lodge Room on January 27, 1871, by M∴W∴William E. Pine, Grand Master, and members of the Grand Lodge.

The following is a list of the Charter Members of the Lodge, together with various data regarding them—listed according to their length of membership in the Lodge:

Name	Master	Date out of Lodge	Reason
Israel Baldwin	(No. 1)	August 21, 1874	Death
Marcus W. Adams	---	April 4, 1876	Demit
Nathan Mingus	1871-2	December 5, 1876	S.N.P.D.
John Whitehead	1873	December 3, 1878*	Demit
George E. P. Howard	1877	March 6, 1883‡	Demit
Samuel Morrow, Jr.	1874	February 8, 1885	Death
Herman P. Witzel	---	June 12, 1916§	Death
George M. Howells	---	December 17, 1900	S.N.P.D.
William M. Clarke	1875	May 21, 1920	Death

*S.N.P.D. Dec. 5, 1876, restored Dec. 3, 1878, demitted same date
‡Demitted April 13, 1874, reaffiliated August 3, 1875
§S.N.P.D. Dec. 2, 1885, restored Jan. 9, 1907

The Tyler, Valentine Aschenbach, was a member and Tyler of Oriental Lodge, No. 51, of Newark.

Thus we find that, of the nine Charter Members, four died, three demitted and two were suspended for the non-payment of dues.

The occupations of these brethren are recorded in the Returns to Grand Lodge as manufacturer, jeweler, bookkeeper, three lawyers, tanner, agent and merchant, in the order listed.

The Officers of the Lodge were:

1. Nathan Mingus .... *Worshipful Master*
2. William M. Clarke .... *Senior Warden*
3. Israel Baldwin, P.M. .... *Junior Warden*
4. John Whitehead .... *Treasurer*
5. Samuel Morrow, Jr. .... *Secretary*
6. George E. P. Howard .... *Senior Deacon*
7. Marcus W. Adams .... *Junior Deacon*
8. Herman P. Witzel ...... *Master of Ceremonies*
9. George M. Howells ...... *Master of Ceremonies*
   Valentine Aschenbach (No. 51) .... *Tyler*

1. Nathan Mingus, the Worshipful Master, was Senior Deacon of St. John's Lodge, No. 1, of Newark, when he demitted to form the new Lodge, but had been Junior Warden the previous year. He was made a Master Mason in the Lodge on February 15, 1865. Demitted January 4, 1871.

2. William M. Clarke, Senior Warden, was also a member of St. John's Lodge, No. 1, but held no office when he demitted, athough he had served the Lodge as a Master of Ceremonies the year before. He was made a Master Mason in the Lodge on September 9, 1868. Demitted January 4, 1871.

3. Israel Baldwin, Junior Warden, had served St. John's Lodge as Worshipful Master in 1868 and 1869. He was made a Master Mason in the Lodge on March 28, 1855. Demitted January 4, 1871.

4. John Whitehead, Treasurer, was made a Master Mason in St. John's Lodge, No. 1, on November 15, 1851, and served as Junior Warden the following year. He demitted in 1856 and affiliated with Franklin Lodge, No. 10, of Irvington, on January 23, 1856. He demitted on December 23, 1864 and affiliated with Cincinnati Lodge, No. 3, of Morristown on March 20, 1865. He was suspended for the non-payment of dues on November 9, 1868 and restored on January 30, 1871 and demitted the same day. He was, therefore, actually under suspension when he signed the petition for Alpha Lodge, and also admitted a Charter Member three days before he

84

was restored to membership. After he demitted from Alpha Lodge on December 3, 1878, his Masonic record ceases, so far as New Jersey is concerned.

5. Samuel Morrow, Jr., Secretary, was made a Master Mason in Solomon's Lodge, No. 46, of Somerville, New Jersey, on September 21, 1864. He was suspended for the non-payment of dues on December 18, 1867 and restored on December 16, 1868, and demitted on the same date. He affiliated with St. John's Lodge, No. 1, on April 7, 1869. Demitted January 4, 1871.

6. George E. P. Howard, Senior Deacon, was made a Master Mason in Eureka Lodge, No. 39, of Newark, New Jersey, on April 6, 1869. He demitted on January 4, 1870 and applied for affiliation in St. John's Lodge, No. 1, but was rejected. As has been shown previously, he became a member of Alpha Lodge and demitted therefrom on March 6, 1883. He affiliated with Roseville Lodge, No. 143, Newark, on April 16, 1883 and on January 30, 1903 demitted from this Lodge. On February 17, 1903 he affiliated with Century Lodge, No. 100, at South Orange, from which he demitted on January 6, 1925, when his Masonic record ceases. (His age then was about 80 years.)

7. Marcus W. Adams, Junior Deacon, was made a Master Mason in St. John's Lodge, No. 1, on October 13, 1869. He was a Master of Ceremonies of the Lodge at the time he demitted, January 4, 1871. He was the first of the Charter members to permanently sever his connection with Alpha Lodge. He accomplished this by demitting on April 4, 1876 after but five years of membership. Five years later, March 9, 1881, he returned to St. John's Lodge, No. 1. On December 12, 1894 he was suspended for the non-payment of dues and restored nine years later, May 13, 1903. He died June 3, 1913, a member of the Lodge.

8. Herman P. Witzel, Master of Ceremonies, was made a Master Mason on December 5, 1864, in Kilwinning Lodge, No. 311, of Chicago, Illinois. He demitted late in 1870. Some time after 1867 he moved to Newark to live.

9. George M. Howells, Master of Ceremonies, was made a Master Mason in 1866 in Cynthia Lodge, No. 155, Cincinnatti, Ohio. He

demitted on March 5, 1869, coming to Newark that same year. At the time of the formation of the Lodge, however, he lived in Flushing, Long Island, N. Y.

Of the nine, but one achieved more than local prominence, Masonically. Worshipful Brother Baldwin became distinguished in two other bodies of Freemasonry in New Jersey.

Christened Israel Beach Baldwin, he never used the middle name or initial. He was born in Newark, New Jersey, on May 5, 1807, and died there on August 21, 1874, being buried on Tuesday, August 25, by Alpha Lodge, No. 116, and several members of Union Chapter, No. 7, Royal Arch Masons.

On May 31, 1859, Brother Baldwin was exalted in Union Chapter, No. 7, R.A.M., of Newark. A couple of years later he was elected Ex. Scribe and the following year became Ex. King. For the next two years (1863 and 1864) he served his Chapter as its Most Excellent High Priest and in 1866 again held the office of Ex. King.

In the Grand Royal Arch Chapter of New Jersey he was elected Grand Royal Arch Captain on September 9, 1863; Grand Captain of the Host on September 14, 1864; and Grand King on September 13, 1865, being admitted and anointed in the Order of High Priesthood on the same evening, and then elected Conductor of the Order. On September 12, 1866, he was elected Most Excellent Grand High Priest of the Grand Royal Arch Chapter. While holding this office, he granted several warrants for new Chapters, among which was one at Newton to be known as Baldwin Chapter (No. 17). He was appointed Grand Lecturer of the Grand Chapter in 1867, 1868 and 1869. In 1870 there appears to have been no such office.

Brother Baldwin was a member of Kane Council, No. 2, Royal and Select Masters, of Newark. He served as Deputy Illustrious Master in 1862 and Thrice Illustrious Master in 1863. At the same time he was in office in the Grand Council of the State. In 1862 he served as Grand Principal Conductor of Work and the following year as Most Illustrious Grand Master.

Israel Baldwin

The records of the St. John Lodge of Perfection list him as 14° in 1868 and in 1875 as "Gr. Orator—deceased."

CHAPTER 4

CHARTER ARRESTED AND RESTORED

ON January 31, 1871, four days after its constitution, Alpha Lodge, No. 116 held its first regular Communication. Petitions for initiation were presented from twelve Negroes, including the original petitioners for "Cushite Lodge"; the Rev. Charles H. Thompson, D.D., who received his Master Mason degree on September 8, 1874: and three others—Davis Brown, William H. DeKalb and William N. Bailey, who were rejected, the first on February 5, 1872 and the other two on February 12, 1872. There was also a petition from one white man, John M. Hoon, a teacher in the Newark Academy, who was the first petitioner elected to membership in the Lodge but who never received any degrees. All of the petitioners were referred to investigating committees.

At this first communication there were several visitors who witnessed the rehearsal of degree work, which no doubt took up the greater part of the evening—it being the first time they had gathered together as an organized lodge, excepting on the evening of constitution.

The Lodge met regularly each week and continued the work of rehearsing degrees. At each communication a few visitors from nearby lodges were present. So far as is known, nothing took place in any way different from the normal business incidental to the early meetings of any lodge. Were it not known, from the petition to Grand Lodge for "Cushite Lodge" that the twelve men who petitioned the Lodge were Negroes, it is doubtful if anyone outside of the Lodge would have known anything about it. The names of these men were known, however, and any visitor at the communication when the petitions were read would be able to impart this information abroad to Freemasons and others, should he so choose. Apparently one or more of these visitors chose to do so.

Brethren in the lodges in and about Newark soon became apprised of the receipt of petitions from Negroes in Alpha Lodge. The Craft and public, generally, became aware of it through the publication of articles in THE LANDMARK, a New York Masonic Weekly (February 11, 18 and 25) and THE NEW YORK SUN (February 21 and 22). The result was a petition to the Grand Master, dated February 24, 1871, signed by two hundred and twelve brethren, which stated, among other things, that it was believed that the Charter of Alpha Lodge was obtained through deceit, etc., and that the Grand Master should take measures to stop the initiation of Negro petitioners in the Lodge, should they be elected.

The M∴W∴Grand Master, in view of the opposition manifested, sent Right Worshipful Brother George B. Edwards (No. 47), Grand Marshal, to the Communication of Alpha Lodge on February 28, with instructions to arrest the Charter. The knowledge of the action of the M∴W∴Grand Master having been spread abroad and, believing that something unusual might happen on the night of the meeting, a large number of visitors were present. In fact, from statements made at different times by some of those who were present, there seems little doubt that the lodge room was filled by the visiting brethren, some of whom, it appears, were Past Masters. As near as the story of what happened can be pieced together from various sources, the following procedure took place. After opening the Lodge and conducting some routine business, the first petition was presented and, upon balloting, the petitioner, Mr. John M. Hoon, was found to be elected. The twelve colored men were then reported upon by the Committees and they were ordered balloted upon. This, however, was not carried out due to immediate subsequent happenings.

One of the brethren was requested to wait on Mr. Hoon and inform him of his election and then request his presence in order that he receive the Entered Apprentice Degree. The brother left the lodge room on his mission.

During his absence Right Worshipful Brother Edwards, Grand Marshal, was announced and received with Grand Honors. He was invited to and received a seat in the East. Upon being called upon he informed the Worshipful Master that he was the bearer of a communication from the M.·.W.·.Grand Master, directed to the Worshipful Master of Alpha Lodge, No. 116. He then read the petition of the variously signed brethren to the Grand Master and then the Grand Master's letter to the Lodge, which amounted, practically, to an order to surrender the Charter to Right Worshipful Brother Edwards. Consequently, in compliance with the Order, the Charter was handed to Right Worshipful Brother Edwards, who closed the Lodge.

Discussion at once appeared in the public press. Some of the articles questioned the right of the Grand Master to order the arrest of the Charter on the grounds of color (although no such reason is actually found in Grand Master Pine's letter). Others upheld his action. Further discussion covered a point that the Grand Marshal had exceeded his authority because the petitioner, Mr. Hoon, was a white man. (The authorization was to secure the charter and was not based on a matter of color.) The LANDMARK (Mar. 4), the NEWARK DAILY JOURNAL (Mar. 11) and the NEWARK DAILY ADVERTISER (Mar. 16) especially participated in "advising" the public of these matters.

As usual, the press muddled up the whole matter. The petition to the Grand Master specifically referred to preventing the initiation of colored men. The Grand Master, however, in his Order to the Lodge, simply authorized Right Worshipful Brother Edwards to secure the Charter, which he ordered surrendered. The matter of color was not mentioned. The Grand Marshal neither exceeded his authority, nor failed in his duty, one which, no doubt, was a very distasteful one for him to perform.

On March 12, 1871, a petition, signed by one hundred and eighty-five (185) brethren was sent to the Grand Master by friends of the Lodge. It requested the Grand Master to convene Grand Lodge and settle the matter by proper Masonic methods—a trial being mentioned, should there be actual charges preferred.

On March 14, 1871, another petition to the Grand Master was sent by the Lodge, which was signed by all of its members. It requested a copy of the original petition read by the Grand Marshal and the

Grand Master's order for the surrender of the Charter, together with any charges which may have been made against the Lodge or its members. According to the Grand Lodge Proceedings, this petition was finally heeded.

The Grand Master committed all matters pertaining to the Lodge to the Committee on Petitions and Grievances on March 30, 1871, and on May 5, the Committee started taking evidence in Oriental Hall, Newark and continued this for four days. Worshipful Brother David L. Garrigus, with counsel, acted for the complainants, and Worshipful Brother Robert Dingwell, with counsel, acted for the defense. They were both members of Eureka Lodge, No. 39, of Newark.

There was considerable legal testimony taken from the witnesses called. The Committee on Dispensations and Warrants reported to Grand Lodge "that the examination of witnesses was continued so long as testimony and evidence were offered or produced on the part of the several petitioners, and until the Committee was informed that no other witnesses would be produced on behalf of either of the petitioners." They also reported "that the representatives and counsel, of the several petitioners, waived making any argument, or furnishing any memoranda of the views of the case as referred, that they entertained, after hearing the testimony produced."

The Master and Wardens of Alpha Lodge and two other members attended the next Annual Communication of Grand Lodge, where M∴W∴William E. Pine, Grand Master, reported in his Annual Address as follows:

"On the evening of the 27th of January, assisted by several of my associate Grand Officers, I constituted and installed the Officers of Alpha Lodge, No. 116, at the city of Newark. On the 24th of the month following, complaint was made to me by Bro. David L. Garrigus [W. M. of Eureka Lodge, No. 39, Newark] and many members of the Grand Lodge, setting forth—among other things—that the warrant of Alpha Lodge was obtained at the last Annual Communication through *deceit* and *misrepresentation*, and that certain proceedings of said Lodge had a tendency to *disturb the peace and harmony* of the Craft in this jurisdiction. After well considering the nature and cause of the complaint I arrested the warrant of said Alpha Lodge.

"I subsequently received a petition from W. Bro. Robert Dingwell [P.M. of Eureka Lodge, No. 39] and others requesting restoration of the warrant, and in the event of refusal to restore the same, to call a special Communication of the Grand Lodge for the purpose of investigating the complaint set forth by the petitioners. Being unauthorized by the facts before me to accede to the first request, and unwilling to call you together for the purpose of considering a complaint which at that time became a matter of reference to a committee, I declined to assemble the Grand Lodge, but referred both petitions and all matters relating thereto, to the Committee on Petitions and Grievances for investigation and report. Upon receipt of the report and evidence, I carefully reviewed the same, and decided to withhold the warrant of Alpha Lodge, No. 116, until this present session of the Grand Lodge. The warrant has been returned to the Grand Secretary, subject to such order as the Grand Lodge shall make. I recommitted the evidence to the Committee on Petitions and Grievances, with instructions to report at the present Communication of the Grand Lodge. The *reports* and *evidence* I submit herewith."

The Committee on Petitions and Grievances reported on this matter and it developed that Worshipful Brother Robert Dingwell, and others had requested the warrant to be restored. All the evidence was read and after considerable discussion, the further consideration of the matter was, on motion, postponed until the evening session.

At eight p.m., the report was called up and after much debate thereon, was agreed to, as follows:

"The Committee on Petitions and Grievances, to whom was referred the evidence taken before this Committee, and all papers having reference to the matter of Alpha Lodge, No. 116, in your favor of December 11th, beg respectfully to say, that they know of no additions that they can make at this time to the report they have already made to the M. W. Grand Master; and further beg leave to hand to him all the papers and report of the Committee in this connection."

The above report was signed by the Committee on January 16, 1872.

"On motion of P. M. Augustus L. Wilcox, of No. 1, that the warrant of Alpha Lodge, No. 116, be restored to said Lodge, was agreed to," by a majority vote of one.

NOTE—The cornerstone of the Newark Academy, mentioned on page 88, was laid on June 25, 1792 by George Washington, president of the United States and William Paterson, Governor of New Jersey.

It was in the foundation for 63 years when in 1855 the building was torn down for a new Post Office building. It was moved to new grounds on High Street, but lost until 1887 when an extension was built, and it was found in the change as being the doorstep. It was then placed on the wall.

CHAPTER 5

FIRST NEGROES MADE FREEMASONS

*A*s soon as the Charter of Alpha Lodge was returned, they set to work. On January 30, 1872, the Rev. John H. L. Sweres and Abram T. Cooke, out of five elected on that date, were initiated, in Oriental Hall, where the Lodge met in the Newark Savings Institution Building. These were the first Negroes to have been initiated into "regular" Freemasonry in New Jersey. They received their Master Mason degree on April 1, 1872, being raised by Worshipful Brother Baldwin. As this was the first time colored brethren had been raised it naturally attracted attention.

According to newspaper accounts over a hundred visitors were present at the communication. The press in Newark carried the story under various headings but featuring the point that they were the first Negroes made Freemasons in New Jersey. Papers in other parts of the country copied the items and some of them added comments of their own. This was especially true in New Jersey and this fact contributed largely in spreading the information to Freemasons in all parts of the State.

In the mean time the Lodge held meetings nearly weekly, so that during the year it elected nine Negro and three white applicants, and initiated, passed and raised them. In addition there were others elected who had received a degree or two by the end of the year. Three Negro applicants were rejected.

The three white men who were admitted, received their Master Mason degrees in the following order—Theodore M. Tucker, May 13; William L. Clawson, July 22; and George Healey, December 16. Clawson became the fifth Master of the Lodge in 1876 and was again Master in 1878, 1880 and 1884. He followed Worshipful Brother Abram T. Cooke, the first colored Master (1879), in 1880 and in 1884 he again followed two colored Masters, Worshipful James H. Baxter (1881 and 1882) and Worshipful Brother Elias S. Ray

(1883). He died on January 18, 1926, and was the last white Master of the Lodge. He held, at various times, many different offices in the Lodge, including Tyler.

The nine colored brethren are listed below according to the date they were made Master Masons in Alpha Lodge, together with information regarding their membership, etc.:

	Name	Age 1872	Occupation
1.	Abram T. Cooke	54	Barber
2.	Rev. John H. L. Sweres	----	Clergyman
3.	John H. O'Fake	53	Music Teacher
4.	James H. Baxter	28	School Principal
5.	Elias S. Ray	30	Bank Janitor
6.	Thomas F. Washington	----	Engineer
7.	Jeremiah G. Evans	32	Engineer
8.	Peter P. O'Fake	51	Dancing Teacher
9.	Alexander Singer	----	Coachman

Master Mason 1872	First Year in Office	W.M.	Date out of Lodge
1. April 7	1875—J.M.C.	1879-85-86	Aug. 4, 1892
2. April 7	---	---	Dec. 2, 1872*
3. April 8	1874—J.W.	---	Jan. 25, 1901
4. April 15	1875—Secty.	1881-82-87 88-92-93	Dec. 28, 1909
5. April 22	1874—J.D.	1883	Aug. 24, 1890
6. April 29	---	---	Oct. 16, 1899‡
7. May 6	1875—S.D.	---	Jan. 8, 1906
8. June 3	---	---	Jan. 28, 1884
9. October 28	1877—J.M.C.	---	Nov. 10, 1901§

All died in membership except Brother Sweres* who demitted and Brother Washington‡ who was suspended for the non-payment of dues. Brother Alexander Singer§ was suspended for the non-payment of dues on December 2, 1885 and restored on January 6, 1896.

CHAPTER 6

THE LODGE BECOMES NEGRO

As mentioned in the previous Chapter, the first initiation of a Negro in Alpha Lodge took place on January 30, 1872. On the same night Trenton Lodge, No. 5, passed a set of Resolutions in which they stated that the admission of persons of color to Freemasonry would be of no benefit to them and would disturb the peace and harmony of the Institution—and requesting the Grand Master to intervene should any Lodge persist in the practice. A copy of these Resolutions was sent to each Lodge in New Jersey.

To show, as an example, the intense activity about the state in regard to this matter, the minutes of a lodge in central New Jersey were examined, and these entries found:

March 5, 1872—"Communications of No. 5 and No. 7 were read and ordered to lay over to the next Regular Communication. It was then moved and seconded that this Lodge indorse the Resolutions of No. 5 and No. 7 in regard to making negro Masons. Moved and seconded that a Committee of three be appointed to Draft resolutions to be sent to the G.L. and all subordinate Lodges in this State. Committee—W.M. appointed Brother R. J. Heywood, L. N. White and W. A. Cole that committee—carried."

March 19, 1872—"Communications were received from Trenton No. 5, Newark No. 7, Olive Branch No. 16, Harmony No. 18, Northern No. 25, Stewart No. 34, Hoboken No. 35, Eureka No. 39 and Alpha No. 116, ordered filed."

April 11, 1872—"Communications from Lodges No. 57, No. 60, No. 63, No. 94, No. 99 were read and ordered filed. Committee on Alpha Lodge matter reported Progress."

June 4, 1872—"Committee on Alpha Lodge matter reported Progress, and four more communications were read and ordered filed."

June 18, 1872—"Moved and seconded that the Committee on Drafts be discharged—carried."

September 3, 1872—"Communication from Trenton No. 5, Princeton No. 38 and Solomon's No. 41 read and ordered filed."

On May 27, 1872, a set of seven charges against Alpha Lodge, No. 116 and its officers was filed in the office of the Grand Secretary. They were read at the Annual Communication on January 22, 1873 and referred to the Committee on Masonic Jurisprudence. On the following day in their report to the Grand Lodge, the Committee completely exonerated those accused and advised that everything done by the Lodge and its officers was in exact accordance with Masonic law and usage. The Grand Lodge approved the Report.

Following this the Resolutions passed by Trenton Lodge, No. 5, were read and declared out of order by the Grand Master.

Prior to this Annual Communication of Grand Lodge, the nine Negro members of Alpha Lodge demitted—December 2, 1872. On the very day that the two happenings above related took place, these nine brethren petitioned Grand Lodge for a warrant for a Lodge to be known as "Surgam Lodge" to be situated in Newark. The word "Surgam" is derived from the Latin "surgo" meaning to erect or rise up.

The petition was recommended by Alpha Lodge. It was referred to the proper committee who advised "that no parties have appeared before the Committee, either to support or oppose the application for said Lodge," etc. They then reported it back to Grand Lodge without recommendation. It was moved to postpone further consideration for a year, but this was rejected by a 207 to 112 vote. The Worshipful Master of Alpha Lodge, W∴Brother John Whitehead, moved that the warrant be issued. The motion was defeated by a vote of 209 to 98. "Surgam Lodge," therefore, never came into existence.

On March 24, 1873, eight of the Negro Brethren reaffiliated with Alpha Lodge. The ninth, the Rev. John H. L. Sweres, had moved back to Ohio. He affiliated there with True American Lodge, No. 2, (Prince Hall) Cincinnati, sometime between June 24, 1873 and June 24, 1874, and was a member until some time between June

24, 1878 and June 24, 1879. In 1874 he is listed as Grand Prelate of the Grand Commandery of Ohio (Prince Hall). He appears as Acting Grand Chaplain in the Grand Chapter of Ohio (Prince Hall) in 1876 and was appointed, in that year, a Deputy Grand High Priest for the State of Kentucky, which was then under the jurisdiction of Ohio. In 1877, in a report, he requested authority to consecrate a Chapter in Louisville, Kentucky, which was granted. He then disappears from the record. He is next heard of in Tennessee. He probably demitted from his Ohio affiliations because of his removal.

Just how Brother Sweres was admitted to True American Lodge would be interesting to know. He no doubt had two demits—one from the Prince Hall Lodge in Newark, or wherever it was that he was made a Prince Hall Mason (probably Kentucky), and the other from Alpha Lodge, No. 116. If he was admitted on the Alpha Lodge demit, he is no doubt the only Negro Brother who ever was admitted into a Prince Hall lodge on a demit issued by a "recognized" lodge of the United States. On the other hand, if he was admitted on a Prince Hall affiliation demit, then he holds the distinction of having been made a Mason in a Prince Hall Lodge, again in a "recognized" lodge, and then returning to another Prince Hall Lodge on a demit from the first one. There are, of course, a number of cases of colored brethren from foreign jurisdictions being affiliated on a demit of a "recognized" lodge. In fact Alpha Lodge, itself had two of them. In Chapter 9 will be found the record of a Negro Brother by the name of Peter S. Henry, who was a member and Secretary of a Fall River, Massachusetts, Lodge. He was formerly a member of Union Lodge (Prince Hall) and because of his initiation in the "regular" lodge was expelled by Union Lodge. This action has been sharply criticized by prominent Prince Hall Freemasons.

At the Annual Election in 1873, two of the Negro Brethren were placed in office. John H. O'Fake was elected Junior Warden and Elias S. Ray was appointed Junior Deacon. On February 9, 1874, following the communication, Past Grand Master William Silas Whitehead addressed the members and their ladies. At the following election on December 22, 1874, a white brother was again elected as Master, Samuel Morrow, Jr. Brother O'Fake, a Negro was elected Treasurer and occupied this office for eighteen years. During the year Deputy Grand Master William A. Pennbrook visited the Lodge and reported it to be in proper working order in the Sixth District.

It was not until the election on December 3, 1878, that the first Negro Master was finally chosen. Brother Abram T. Cooke, the first Negro initiate, was elected, and thus became the first Negro Master in the United States in a "recognized" lodge. Brothers Baxter and Ray, also Negro brethren, were the Wardens.

Nearly all of the candidates after this date were colored men and the white brethren soon began to fall from the membership through death, demit and suspension for the non-payment of dues. In a few years all of the officers were Negroes and the Lodge thus became a "mixed" lodge so far as color is concerned. The last four white brethren in the Lodge were Worshipful Brother William M. Clarke, who was the first Senior Warden and the fourth Worshipful Master, who died on May 21, 1920, Worshipful Brother William L. Clawson, who died on January 18, 1926, and Louis Rich and Magliore A. Lapointe who were suspended for the non-payment of dues on November 14, 1929.

For many years the lodge did not participate in the District Lodge of Instruction nor the District Grand Lodge of Instruction, but was examined separately by the District Deputy at a regular communication of the Lodge. Early in the twentieth century, however, the Lodge attended the District meeting and soon afterward began attending Grand Lodge of Instruction. Other than this, the Lodge has in every way worked as other subordinate lodges under the Grand Lodge of New Jersey have done.

Being the only "recognized" colored lodge in the United States, it naturally has more than its share of visitors. Those who have visited have always reported being fraternally received and when there has been "work" it has been well up to the standard of the degree work of the Jurisdiction.

CHAPTER 7

RELATIONSHIPS WITH OTHER
GRAND LODGES

$\mathcal{A}$ T the June 27, 1872, Annual Communication of the Grand Lodge of Delaware, M∴W∴J. C. McCabe, Grand Master, in his Annual Address, recommended that Delaware lodges should be instructed not to have Masonic intercourse with Alpha Lodge, Nó. 116 of New Jersey. Grand Lodge approved and the lodges in Delaware were so instructed. Several other Grand Jurisdictions criticised this action of the Grand Lodge of Delaware in the "mind your own business" attitude, although some of these, too, did not approve of the "making" of Negro Masons.

In Mississippi, M∴W∴W. H. Hardy, Grand Master, after some correspondence with the Grand Master of New Jersey, informed his Grand Lodge in 1873 about the subject in an adverse manner but with no recommendation. The Committee on Foreign Correspondence recommended a severance of fraternal relations but wiser members of Grand Lodge were successful in getting a Resolution passed, as follows:

> "That the M. W. Grand Lodge of Masons in New Jersey has been found adequate to deal with the question of admitting Negroes into membership with its subordinate Lodges and it is the confident expectation of this Grand Lodge that she also will be found adequate to meet the emergency presented by the action of Alpha Lodge, No. 116 of Newark, N. J."

For thirty-five years no change in the situation took place, when, without warning, a letter was received by the Grand Master of New Jersey, M∴W∴William D. WolfsKeil, from the Grand Master of Mississippi, M∴W∴Edwin J. Martin, in August, 1908, which stated that he "had heard that there is a lodge in your Grand Jurisdiction composed of negroes, and that your Grand Lodge permits the initiation and affiliation of negroes as Masons." M∴W∴Brother Martin requested to be advised if this was true.

"I at once replied," said M∴W∴Brother WolfsKeil, "supposing the inquiry to have been prompted by personal curiosity, which I had satisfied by a brief relation of the facts in regard to our Alpha Lodge, No. 116. After an interval of several months, I received this letter:" (extract)

"Yours of August 25th., advising me that negroes are initiated and affiliated in your Grand Jurisdiction is received.

"Our Grand Lodge hold differently. Masonry never contemplated that her privileges should be extended to a race, totally morally and intellectually incapacitated to discharge the obligations which they assume or have conferred upon them in a Masonic Lodge. It is no answer that there are exceptions to this general character of the race. We legislate for the race and not for the exceptions.

"We hold that affiliation with negroes is contrary to the teachings of Masonry, and is dangerous to the interest of the Fraternity of Free and Accepted Masons.

"Therefore, I, E. J. Martin, Grand Master of Masons in the State of Mississippi, do order that fraternal correspondence between the Grand Lodge of Mississippi and the Most Worshipful Grand Lodge of New Jersey be and is hereby discontinued until such time as the Most Worshipful Grand Lodge of New Jersey shall see fit to desist from her present practice of initiating and affiliating negroes as Masons.

"With my best personal regards, I am, sincerely yours,

(Signed) Edwin J. Martin, Grand Master."

Most Worshipful Brother WolfsKeil then gave a brief summary of the history of the Lodge, preceded by this paragraph:

"Some of the correspondence between Grand Masters is prompted by an overburdening sense of responsibility for the good conduct of the Craft, often enough outside of their own jurisdiction, and common courtesy suggests that such instances of emotional activity be kept where they belong, in the private records of the Grand Master."

Near the end of the summary is to be found this paragraph:

"Of the conduct of administration of the affairs of Alpha Lodge, after its warrant had been returned to it, no one now alive may justly offer criticism. It may be safely assumed that every Grand Master succeeding M.'.W.'.William E. Pine, kept that lodge under watchful supervision, and became satisfied that every petitioner for membership was dealt with in literal and exact conformity to the rules of this Grand Lodge and the regulations governing the Craft."

And so the Grand Lodge let the matter stand. At the Annual Communication of the Grand Lodge of Mississippi in 1909, M.'.W.'. Brother Martin reported his action to Grand Lodge and a Special Committee of five had the matter referred to them. At the Annual Communication in 1910 this Committee made their report to Grand Lodge—a matter of two printed pages in the proceedings (105 and 106)—wherein the Grand Lodge supported the action of the Grand Master. (Page 120).

Let us now turn to page 32 of the 1927 Proceedings of the Grand Lodge of Mississippi and excerpt a paragraph from the address of M.'.W.'.John R. Tally:

"Whereas, from a careful reading from the correspondence between the Grand Master of New Jersey and our Past Grand Master Ed Martin, at the time fraternal relations were severed between this Grand Jurisdiction and New Jersey, I am convinced that the true situation was not understood by either of the Grand Masters. And, whereas, all other States that severed relations with New Jersey at the same time have long since resumed fraternal relations with that sister Jurisdiction, Therefore, I think that the time has arrived when we should forget this difference and resume fraternal relations with the Grand Jurisdiction of New Jersey."

Without going into further technical details, suffice it for our purpose to say that M.'.W.'.James Henry Johnson, in his report to the Grand Lodge in 1928, (page 41 of Proceedings) informed the Grand Lodge of Mississippi that he had personally talked to the Grand Master of New Jersey and arranged that the two Jurisdictions would resume their former fraternal relations and that the Grand Master of New Jersey, at his invitation, was then present and would address Grand Lodge.

Most Worshipful Howard R. Cruse, Grand Master of New Jersey, was introduced and acclaimed loudly. He then addressed the Grand Lodge of Mississippi and was warmly applauded (Pages 67 to 74 of 1928 Proceedings.)

On April 17, 1929, M∴W∴George D. Riley, Past Grand Master of Mississippi, returned the visit and was received with Grand Honors by Grand Lodge, where he delivered a stirring address to the brethren assembled, that will be long remembered by those who were privileged to hear it. Thus closed the so-called "Mississippi incident."

At the first Annual Communication of the Grand Lodge of Oklahoma on February 9, 1910, the Grand Master announced that he had not requested fraternal correspondence with the Grand Lodge of New Jersey, being in sympathy with the brethren in Mississippi. Four years later, however, this Grand Lodge reversed its former stand and fraternal relations were entered into with New Jersey.

In some other Grand Jurisdictions considerable discussion ensued on the question, nothing of importance came of it and as time went on the whole matter ceased to be of moment and has long since been forgotten.

CHAPTER 8

ALPHA LODGE NO. 116, STATISTICS

*T*HAT the story of Alpha Lodge, No. 116, may be complete, certain statistical computations are herein recorded, because stories regarding the membership of the Lodge are often as far from the truth as are other alleged historical facts connected with the Lodge. All data were obtained from the Returns of Alpha Lodge to the Grand Lodge.

There have been exactly 198 members of the Lodge since the date of its Charter in 1871 to the end of the year 1938. The classification of the membership is as follows:

Living members	79	Charter members	9
S.N.P.D.	58	Raised	187
Died	54	Affiliated	2
Demitted	7		
		Total	198
Total	198	S.N.P.D. (restored)	8
E. A. only	4	Demit and re-aff.	9

The affiliates were No. 110 from Scotia Lodge, No. 340, Barbados, British West Indies and No. 142 from Unity Lodge, No. 797, Georgetown, British Guiana. Both of these Lodges are on the Register of the Grand Lodge of Scotland. Including the Charter Members, 19 have been white, 176 Negroes, 2 Indians, and 1 Hindu.

Only three final rejections are recorded, one on February 5, 1872 and two on February 12, 1872, although others were rejected, applied subsequently and were elected to membership.

Daniel W. Clark, (No. 74) was previously a member of Hiram Lodge, No. 23 (Prince Hall) of Brooklyn, New York, where he received the Entered Apprentice and Fellowcraft Degrees on May 11, 1901 and the Master Mason Degree on May 18, 1901. He was Master of the Lodge in 1904. He became a Master Mason in Alpha Lodge, No. 116, on March 13, 1907.

John W. Dias (No. 80) was made an Entered Apprentice on July 4, a Fellowcraft on August 15, and a Master Mason on September 19, 1905, in Carthaginian Lodge, No. 47 (Prince Hall) of Brooklyn, New York. On December 1, 1908, he wrote to the Lodge and asked how he could sever all connection with it and was told by paying his dues to date and asking for a demit. As no further record of him is to be found in Carthaginian Lodge prior to the date he became a Master Mason in Alpha Lodge (March 10, 1909) he probably had no further contact with that Lodge.

During the sixty-eight years of the existence of the Lodge there have been thirty-two Masters—one served for ten years; one, six years; one, four years; six, three years; seven, two years and sixteen, one year.

There have been nine Secretaries serving 2, 2, 20, 2, 11, 3, 15, 5 and 8 years in the order of their election.

The average membership by blocks of years is as follows:

Charter year	9	average 9.0 per year
7 years	20	2.9
20 years	15	0.8
20 years	53	2.7
20 years	101	5.1
—	—	—
68 years	198	2.9

Subtracting years when none were raised:

Charter year	9	average 9.0 per year
4 years	20	5.0
9 years	15	1.7
18 years	53	2.9
19 years	101	5.4
—	—	—
51 years	198	3.9

There were never any suspensions for un-Masonic conduct nor any expulsions for any reason.

CHAPTER 9

NEGRO MASONS IN OTHER WHITE LODGES AFTER 1870

*A*T the beginning of this historical recital instances of Negroes being made Masons in white lodges were cited. No appreciable increase in these "makings" has ever occurred. We report here a few cases to show that there have been Negro Masons in "recognized" white lodges up to the present time.

GREENSBURG LODGE, No. 36, Greensburg, Indiana—John W. Thurman, a Negro, was Initiated February 2, 1875, Passed March 2, 1875, and Raised April 9, 1875. Installed Junior Deacon January 5, 1880 he served in that office for six years, during which time he made a specialty of instructing candidates in learning the Lectures. He died on September 2, 1896, a member of the Lodge.

MOUNT HOPE LODGE, Fall River, Massachusetts—Peter S. Henry, a Negro, was born in Richmond, Virginia on December 15, 1853. He was elected to receive the degrees of Masonry in Mount Hope Lodge on March 3, 1882, Entered May 12, Passed June 16, Raised July 14, and signed the By-Laws on the same day. At that time he was a bank clerk. He was Secretary of the Lodge in 1893 and 1894 and declined re-election. He died on May 16, 1913, a member of the Lodge.

ST. ANDREW'S LODGE, Boston, Massachusetts—Joshua Bowen Smith, a Negro, was born in Coatsville, Pennsylvania, on November 3, 1813 and came North in 1836 and settled in Cambridge, Massachusetts. He was entered on October 10, 1867, Passed on November 14, and Raised on December 12 in St. Andrew's Lodge. In those days it was the custom for lodges to make Masons and consider their application for membership separately. Brother Smith did not affiliate with St. Andrew's Lodge but on January 16, 1872, he affiliated with Adelphi Lodge, South Boston. He was a very renowned caterer at the time. He became a Warden of his Lodge and thus a member

Some of the members of the Williams & Walker Company made Master Masons in Waverly Lodge,

of the Grand Lodge of Massachusetts during his term of office. He represented the City of Cambridge in the State Legislature in 1873 and 1874.

Brother Smith was made a Royal Arch Mason in St. Matthews Royal Arch Chapter, South Boston on June 14, 1869. He was Knighted in St. Omer Commandery, K.T., South Boston, November 15, 1869.

In the Ancient and Accepted Scottish Rite, Brother Smith was given the degrees from the 4th to the 14th, on May 21, 1869 in Boston Lodge of Perfection, by Communication. He received the 17th and 18th degrees in full ceremonial form on the same date in Mt. Olivet Chapter of Rose Croix, Boston. These dates are taken directly from the minute books of the two bodies. There are no extant records of this period for Boston Council, Princes of Jerusalem, but he must have had the 15th and 16th degrees communicated to him in that Council the same night or he would not have been able to take the degrees in the Chapter without them. The records of the Supreme Council show that he was made a 32nd Degree Mason on the same date in Boston Sovereign Consistory and his name is listed in the Proceedings of the Supreme Council in the report of the Deputy. A roster of members of Massachusetts Consistory (a combination of Boston, De Witt Clinton and Massachusetts Consistories) dated 1877 shows him listed as a member.

There is an extended Memorial of him in the records of Boston Lodge of Perfection, dated November 24, 1879. He had died July 5, 1879.

This is the only record which shows a Negro in a white Chapter, Commandery and Consistory. References to him are to be found in the Boston newspapers of December 1, 1867 and in *"The Lodge of St. Andrew and the Massachusetts Grand Lodge"* 1870.

Brother Smith was not the only Negro initiated in St. Andrew's Lodge. At the Annual Communication of the Grand Lodge of Massachusetts (white) in 1871, Grand Master William Sewall Gardner "presented the application of Alfred R. Lewis and seven others of Boston, for a Dispensation for a new Lodge, to be called Thistle Lodge, and stated that the circumstances of this petition were such, that he desired to take the advice of the Grand Lodge upon the propriety of granting the same. R∴W∴Sereno D. Nickerson moved that the petition, not being in proper form, the petitioners have leave to withdraw, and, after full discussion, the motion prevailed." (See page 252, Proceedings of the Grand Lodge of Massachusetts, 1871).

SIMONDS LODGE, No. 59, Shoreham, Vermont—Brother William J. Anderson, a Negro, was raised in Simonds Lodge, No. 59, on November 24, 1898. He was Secretary of the Lodge from June 1931 to June 1932. Previous to that he had been Chaplain of the Lodge for three years. He declined re-election as Secretary after the single term. This brother is the only colored man we have found, at the present, in membership in a white lodge in the United States.

A CANADIAN COLORED LODGE—It is our purpose to confine our remarks to Freemasonry in the United States. However, there has frequently been brought out that there are or were colored Freemasons or a lodge in Nova Scotia, Canada, in recent times. It is, therefore, briefly mentioned here.

In 1855, five colored men were initiated in Royal Sussex Lodge, No. 6, of Halifax. They subsequently applied to the Hon. Alexander Keith, the District Grand Master of the District Grand Lodge of England in Nova Scotia, for a Dispensation. This was granted and a Charter was issued on December 3, 1856, by the Grand Lodge of England, numbered 994. The number was changed to 693 in 1863. In 1869 the Lodge joined the Grand Lodge of Nova Scotia and was assigned the number 18.

For many years it did good work, when it was in the hands of capable brethren and when they confined their candidates to men of Color. About 1910, however they started accepting petitions from any man, and no matter where he resided, whether in Nova Scotia or British Columbia, and occasionally from the United States. About this time the Secretary got short in his accounts too. After an investigation by Grand Lodge, the Charter was forfeited in June, 1916, and the Lodge has not functioned since.

The members in good standing were given demits-at-large and one or two of them affiliated with other lodges.

APPENDIX

[I]

GRAND LODGES OF NEGRO FREEMASONS

1791—Massachusetts
1815—Pennsylvania
1845—New York and Maryland
1848—District of Columbia and New Jersey
1849—Ohio and Delaware
1855—California
1856—Indiana and Rhode Island
1863—Louisiana
1865—Michigan and Virginia
1866—Kentucky and Missouri
1867—Illinois, South Carolina and Kansas
1870—North Carolina, Florida, Georgia, Tennessee and Alabama
1872—Mississippi
1873—Arkansas
1874—Connecticut and Ontario, Canada
1875—Texas
1876—Colorado
1877—West Virginia
1887—Iowa
1893—Oklahoma
1894—Minnesota
1903—Washington
1919—Nebraska
1920—Arizona
1921—New Mexico
1925—Wisconsin

[II]

NATIONAL COMPACT GRAND LODGE

"The Most Worshipful National Grand Lodge of Free and Accepted Ancient York Masons of Color, for the United States of North America, and the Masonic jurisdiction thereunto belonging."

Established	June 23, 24, 25, 26, 28, 1847, Boston, Mass.
	June 25, 1848
	Oct. 13, 1848 New York. City
	June 25, 26, 27, 28, 29, 1849 Philadelphia, Pa.
1st Triennial	June 21, 22, 23, 24, 25, 1850
2nd Triennial	July, 1853
	Mar. 31, 1854 Philadelphia, Pa.
3rd Triennial*	July 7, 8, 9, 10, 11, 12, 14, 21, 1856 Philadelphia, Pa.
4th Triennial	August 4, 1859 Cincinnati, Ohio
	July 4, 1860 Pittsburg, Pa. (adjourned Session)
5th Triennial*	Oct. 7, 8, 9, 1862 New York, N. Y.
6th Triennial*	Oct. 16, 17, 18, 19, 20, 21, 23, 24, 25, 26, 27, 1865 Baltimore, Maryland.
7th Triennial	Oct. 5, 1868
	Oct. 9, 1869 Wilmington, Del.
8th Triennial	Oct. 1871 Chicago, Illinois
	March, 1873 Philadelphia, Pa.
9th Triennial*	May 11, 12, 13, 14, 15, 1874 Louisville, Kentucky
	June 23, 24, 1875 Boston, Mass. (P.H.G.L. called)
10th Triennial	May 16, 1877 Pittsburg, Pa. (last regular meeting)
	Sept. 4, 1877 Chicago, Illinois (called by independent members of 21 jurisdictions)
	1877 Wilmington, Delaware. (organization voided)
	May 8, 1878—Announcement of final meeting Wilmington, Del.—never held.

(*) Have printed Proceedings—G. L. of Iowa has copies.

[III]

NATIONAL GRAND MASTERS AND NATIONAL GRAND SECRETARIES

NATIONAL COMPACT GRAND LODGE

YEAR	NATIONAL GRAND MASTER
1847	John T. Hilton (Mass.)
1850	Enos A. Hall (Pa.)
1856	William Darnes (Ohio)

110

1862	Paul Drayton, (N. Y.)
1865	Richard H. Cleaves (Pa.)
1868	Richard H. Cleaves (Pa.)
1871	Richard H. Cleaves (Pa.)
1874	Richard H. Cleaves (S. C.)
1877	Richard H. Cleaves (S. C.)

YEAR	NATIONAL GRAND SECRETARY
1847	William E. Ambush (Mass.)
1850	James J. Richmond (Pa.)
1856	Rev. Samuel W. Chase, Sr. (Md.)
1862	Edward M. Thomas (D. of C.)
1865	Dr. Jonathan Davis (Pa.)
1868	?
1871	?
1874	George W. Le Vere (Tenn.)
1877	?

William E. Ambush subsequently became a member of the Grand Lodge of Ohio.

Enos A. Hall subsequently moved to New York

Richard H. Cleaves was a Past Grand Master of the Grand Lodge of Ohio but was a resident of Pennsylvania when elected National Grand Master. He moved to South Carolina and was prominent in Masonry there when elected for the fourth time as National Grand Master. Later he moved to the District of Columbia and was active Masonically there.

Dr. Jonathan Davis was prominent in every branch of Masonry in the Grand bodies of Pennsylvania and was the head of Adoptive Masonry at least as early as 1872 and for a number of years afterward. His son, now a rather elderly man, is still identified with the Craft in Philadelphia.

[IV]

THE CHILLICOTHE WARRANT

To All Whom It may Concern Throughout The Globe
Send Greeting:

111

Know ye, That we the Grand Lodge of the State of Ohio formed at the town of Chillicothe, in the year of our Lord 1808, A.Y.M. 5808, of the most ancient and honorable fraternity of free and accepted Ancient York Masons, according to the old institution duly established and organized for the said State by a resolution, and by the authority of a convention of ancient York Masons held at Chillicothe, State of Ohio, do hereby constitute and authorize and appoint our trusty and well beloved brethren, James Miller, Worshipful Master; John Matthews, Senior Warden, and George W. Hilton, Junior Warden, of a new Lodge denominated Harmony Lodge, No. 5, to be held in the City of Philadelphia. We do hereby authorize and empower our trusty and well beloved brethren, James Miller, John Mathews and George W. Hilton to hold their Lodge at the place hereby appointed and directed, at such times as they may think necessary according to the rule of Masonry, and to admit and make Free Masons according to the most ancient and honorable custom of the Royal craft in all ages and nations throughout the known world and not contrarywise; we do further authorize and empower our said brethren, James Miller, John Mathews and George W. Hilton to hear and determine all and singular, matters and things relating to the craft within their respective jurisdiction of the said Lodge. And lastly we do hereby authorize and empower our trusty and well beloved brethren to nominate, choose and pass, and to install their successors from time to time, and such successors shall in like manner install their successors to office to whom they shall deliver this warrant, and such installation to be upon Saint John's the Evangelist days, during the continuance of this Lodge, forever.

Given under the hands and seal of the Grand Lodge for the State of Ohio, May 7, 1833, A.L. 5833.

> Conrad Ferguson, M.W.G.M.
> Robert Stephenson, R.W.D.G.M.
> Henry Voight, R.W.S.G.W.
> James Wilson, R.W.J.G.W.
> Jonathan Battorf, R.W.G.T.
> Wilson Hunter, R.W.G.S.

[V]
PRINCE SAUNDERS

In the Massachusetts Historical Society there is a manuscript auto-biography of William Bentley Fowle, in which we find that Prince Saunders (Sanders), who was initiated in African Lodge in 1809, and who was its Secretary in 1811, is mentioned as follows:

"He became engaged to a daughter of Paul Cufee, a colored sea Captain of New Bedford, who owned several vessels . . . . . he persuaded his friends to subscribe enough to enable him to go to London [1812-1813]. Previously to going, he released Miss Cufee from his engagement . . . . . He carried good letters to England, and going as a delegate of the Masonic lodge of Africans, who held their charter from England, he became acquainted with the Royal Duke, who was at the head of the craft there, and immediately was introduced to the highest circles. The nobility walked arm in arm with him in the streets of London."

Saunders was baptized in Lebanon, Connecticut in 1784 and in 1805 is listed as a property owner in Lebanon. He was educated in a local academy under the patronage of a white lawyer, taught a colored school at Colchester, Connecticut, and was a student at Dartmouth, 1807-8. President John Wheelock recommended him as a teacher in the African School in Boston, held at the home of Primus Hall, who was a member of African Lodge, also.

In England, Saunders met Wilberforce and at his suggestion went to Haiti, where he set up a school system under Emperor Christophe. The latter made him a special envoy to England, and while there he published "Haitian Papers" a translation of the laws with his commentaries. About 1818 he was recalled but came to Philadelphia instead, where he affiliated with the African Lodge there. In 1820, after Christophe's death, he returned to Haiti and was made Attorney General by President Boyer. Saunders died at Port-au-Prince, Haiti in 1839.

Inquiries in England do not shed any light on his visit there, Masonically. There are no "letter books" extant covering the period 1791-1818 in the Grand Lodge of England.

[VI]

PETITION OF LEWIS HAYDEN (P.H.) AND OTHERS
TO GRAND LODGE OF MASSACHUSETTS (WHITE)
(Annual Communication Grand Lodge of Massachusetts
December 9, 1869—page 454-463).

A full record of this matter will be found in the Proceedings of the Grand Lodge of Massachusetts (white) from which we extract this portion of the Committee's report.

"The petitioners do not avowedly represent either of these Lodges [Master Masons of Boston; members of Union Lodge, No. 7, New Bedford; and members of Sumner Lodge, No. 12, Springfield] or any others; so that their statements and prayer should be regarded as expressions of individual persons, rather than the representations and request of the Lodges mentioned in the petition. . . . .

"Our Constitution makes no distinction on account of the color of persons who desire the benefits of Freemasonry, and there are no rules or regulations whereby the petitioners, if worthy and well qualified,' are excluded from our fraternity, if they seek admission through duly organized Lodges.

"Our Committee recommend that the petitioners have leave to withdraw.

> Signed—Heard, Warren, Wales, Wright, Moore, Cheever, Woodbury."

The report of the Committee was "accepted."

[VII]

RICHARD P. G. and THEODORE S. WRIGHT

RECORDS OF ST. GEORGE'S LODGE, No. 6, Schenectady, N. Y.

Richard P. G. Wright, Hairdresser. Affiliated, March 28, 1844. Died, May 29, 1847.

Theodore S. Wright, Clergyman. Affiliated, August 28, 1844. Died, March 25, 1847.

RETURNS OF ST. GEORGE'S LODGE, No. 6,—June 24, 5843 to June 24, 5844

No. 2299 (No. 19 in Lodge) Richard P. G. Wright, residing in Schenectady, joined March 28, 1844.

RETURNS OF ST. GEORGE'S LODGE, No. 6—June 1, 5844
to June 1, 5845

No. 3309 (No. 26 in Lodge) Theodore S. Wright, residing in Schenectady. Born in Schenectady, age 44. Clergyman. Joined August 28, 1844. Initiated in Morton Lodge, No. 87.

The "Schenectady Reflector," June 11, 1847

"In New York on the 29th, ult, [died] Mr. Richard P. G. Wright, of this city, in the 75th year of his age. Father of the late Rev. Theodore S. Wright."

The "Schenectady Reflector," April 2, 1847

"In New York, March 25, [died] in the full hope of a blessed immortality, Rev. Theodore Sedgwick Wright, Pastor of the 1st Colored Presbyterian Church in that city in the 50th year of his age."

DOCUMENTS Respecting the Controversy Between The Grand Lodge of Hamburg and New York. Sec. V. page 17, letter from R. Barthelmess, W. M. of Pythagoras Lodge, No. 1, Brooklyn:

"Colored brethren have also been admitted in Pythagoras Lodge, when it bore the number 86 and was a subordinate of the Gr. Lodge of New York. The minutes of the meeting of the 15th of January 1847, proves the presence, among the visitors, of the colored brother and clergyman Wright, member of St. George's Lodge, No. 6 in Schenectady, a subordinate of the white men's Gr. Lodge of the State of New York . . . . . Br. Wright, here alluded to, together with his son, had, in several instances, visited."

The references to the son, should, of course, be the father—but the document shows that they both visited the Lodge in Brooklyn.

PROCEEDINGS OF N. Y. COUNCIL OF DELIBERATION (Scottish Rite) 1902, page 152-153:

"The following brethren received the Ineffable Degrees in the Old Lodge of Perfection . . . . . revived A.D. 1821, in the City of Schenectady, N. Y.:

Richard P. G. Wright—late Tyler in L. of P. K. Temp.
Highest Degree received—Perfection.
Residence—Schenectady, N. Y.
Born—March 5, 1776 in Bristol, Mass. [now Maine]
Occupation—Hairdresser
Religion—Protestant
(Wright's name is the 5th on the list)

SAME, 1902—page 138
"On Sept. 7, 1822, the following officers were installed:
R. P. G. Wright—G. Treasurer"

SAME, 1914—page 284
"On November 11, 1823, the following officers were elected:
R. P. G. Wright, Tiler"

SAME, 1902—page 138
"The following is a list of members of the Lodge [of Perfection]
on September 22, 1841:
Richard P. G. Wright, G. E. P. & S. M., and P. of J."

SAME, 1902—page 140
"At the annual meeting held September 23, 1841, the follow-
ing officers were elected and installed:
Richard P. G. Wright—Grand Tyler."

When this data is consolidated we have:

RICHARD P. G. WRIGHT, Hairdresser, born March 5, 1776 in Bristol,
Mass. Resident of Schenectady, N. Y. Made a Freemason at least as
early as 1821, he having received grades in a Lodge of Perfection in
that year. Member as late as September 23, 1841. Affiliated St.
George's Lodge, No. 6, Schenectady, N. Y., on March 28, 1844.
Moved to New York, N. Y. Visited Pythagoras Lodge, No. 86,
Brooklyn, N. Y., several times. Died New York, May 29, 1847,
aged 71 years (newspaper says 74 years).

THEODORE SEDGWICK WRIGHT, Clergyman, and graduate of Princeton College, born 1800 in Schenectady, N. Y. Resident of Schenectady, N. Y. Made a Freemason in Morton Lodge, No. 87 some time
after 1821 and lodge became dormant shortly thereafter. Affiliated
St. George's Lodge, No. 6, Schenectady, N. Y., on August 28, 1844.

Moved to New York, N. Y. Visited Pythagoras Lodge, No. 86, Brooklyn, N. Y. several times. Died New York, March 25, 1847, aged 47 years (newspaper says 49 years).

[VIII]
R. P. G. Wright Lodge No. 20 (Prince Hall)
Schenectady, N. Y.

A rather odd circumstance is that the National Compact Grand Lodge of New York chartered the above lodge as number 29 on January 27, 1869. At the consolidation of the National Union Grand Lodge of New York with the United Grand Lodge of New York in 1878, a new warrant was issued dated December 18, 1878, with the number 20. The lodge is now dormant.

Brother Wright was a member of St. George's Lodge, No. 6, (white) of Schenectady and must have been a prominent citizen of Schenectady among both races. Even though he was a member of a white lodge the Negro brethren must have considered him very highly to erect a lodge of their own in his memory.

[IX]

Letter in Archives of Grand Lodge of New York (White)
"New York, Dec. 26th, 1851

Jas. W. Powell, M.D. [Grand Secretary of the Grand Lodge of New York (white)]

Dear Sir:

With the compliments of the festive Season permit me to inform you that I have been instructed to communicate to you as the Grand Secretary of the Grand Lodge of the State of New York, that the 'United Grand Lodge of the State of New York' composed of Colored Free Masons have addressed a Communication to the Honourable Body for which you act, together with a copy of their Constitution and Articles of Union which I herewith transmit. I have also enclosed in the same, a copy of the Constitution, etc. for the Grand Officers of your Grand Lodge, whose names are subscribed thereon, and in consequence of not having their address you will confer a great favor by forwarding them to their respective destinations, sincerely hoping that after a perusal of the Communication you will be favorably impressed to our feeble efforts in the cause of Masonic Unity and give us your aid in council in our pursuit after 'Light' is the earnest and sincere desire of yours in the 'Mystic Tie.'

RANSOM F. WAKE
Grand Sec. of The U.G.L. of the S. of N.Y."

[X]

LETTER IN ARCHIVES OF GRAND LODGE OF NEW YORK (WHITE)
"Binghamton, [N. Y.] Oct. 2nd, 1859

Mr. Austin, Sir: (G. S.)

I want to make some inquiries of you with respect to the relation between the White Masons & Colored Masons of the State of New York or rather I want to [know] what we can do (we colored Masons of Binghamton). In the Spring of 1853 Joseph P. Turner, Moore Walker and others purporting to be grand officers of the Philanthropic Grand Lodge of New York, established a Lodge in this place. We men of color were children and ignorant of Masonic Law and usage and of its arbitrary nature. We were furnished with a dispensation and afterwards a charter bearing the date of Sept. 23, A.L. 5853 but we soon found we were misled. So we have been working on our own hook for some time past. We have a good room and some furniture. We have been regularly Entered, Passed and Raised. We have seen both points of the Compass. What we want is to become subordinate to the Grand Lodge of this jurisdiction and what I wish to inquire is how or what steps we can take or what means we can use, to and to do. You will do me a great favor to drop me a few lines and let me know.

Yours,

MORRIS J. WILKINS"

On the back is "Morris J. Wilkins (colored) Recd. Oct. 5/59
—a little mixed"

There were four Grand Lodges of Negro Masonry in New York in 1859: The United Grand Lodge; the Grand Lodge of New York, National Union; the Osiris Electic Grand Lodge of North America;

118

and the Philanthropic Grand Lodge. The last two were operating out of the State also. In 1858, letters were exchanged in an attempt at consolidation of the three bodies. Nothing appears to have come out of the attempt, the minutes of the United Grand Lodge showing the last meeting of the Philanthropic Grand Lodge in 1860.

[XI]

LETTER IN ARCHIVES OF GRAND LODGE OF NEW YORK (WHITE)
"Salisbury, N. C.

M.W.G.M. of Masons of New York.

Brother:

Some time since I saw an extract from the "Anglo African" a paper published in New York to the effect that Past M.·.W.·. Paul Drayton of the National Grand Lodge is about to resume his labors of organizing Lodges in the South under the authority of the M.W.G.L. of New York, and I also saw it stated in a New Berne (N. C.) paper that a Lodge of Negroes has been formed in that City composed of Negroes. The "Anglo African" states that M.·.W.·. P. Drayton was about to organize King Solomon's Lodge in New Berne and this New Berne paper said that such was the name of the Negro Lodge. Most Masons have supposed that the secrets of our order had been imparted unlawfully by your *authority*—that is to say, by the formation of a Lodge within our jurisdiction empowered to receive negroes who had been former slaves. I could not, and yet do not believe that any of our northern brethren could so far use the virtue of the order as to sanction much less enjoy the admission into our fraternity of those who were not *free born*—nor could I or do I believe that any Grand Lodge, but more especially that of New York, would attempt to charter any *local* Lodge within the borders of our State or if the expression be preferred, within the territory limits of our Grand Lodge jurisdiction, which is that of the State or what at least was formerly the State. There is no Grand Lodge which can complain more justly of a similar infraction of Grand Lodge jurisdiction. In the chartering of Pythagoras Lodge the Grand Lodge of Hamburg invaded your jurisdiction and insulted your Grand Lodge—you complained and many if not every Grand Lodge sided with you, among others North Carolina. The subject underwent a thorough discussion and the action of the G.L. of Hamburg met with the condemnation of the whole Masonic fraternity over the world. I had thought that perhaps the negroes North had formed a benevolent order taking our name and that it was thought fitting to encourage them to persevere in so laudable a work as distinct from thorough assimilation in principles to our Order and I can see no objection to that. To do good is right whether it proceeds from white or black but we cannot admit the negroes, formerly slaves, to our order, *even if we would*—Having premised this much, I respectfully request you, in brotherly kindness, to inform me whether we are to understand the articles in their full meaning, and if not, what we are to understand. Hoping to hear from you soon, I am,

Fraternally yours, etc.

(Signed) W. H. BAILEY"

Another letter attached to the above

"Salisbury, N. C.

Jan. 22/66

Dear Sir and Brother:

I have the honor herewith to enclose a letter from Past Master Bailey, of this place, addressed to the M.W.G.M. of Masons of your State. I have been so fortunate as to obtain your name and address from a young gentleman here, a member of your Lodge and take the liberty of requesting you to forward the enclosed to the M. W. Grand Master of Masons—New York—as his address is unknown to us. The subject of the letter is one of interest to us all. As an officer of the United States I do not have any prejudices against the Negro—but as a Mason and a member of a North Carolina Chapter, I do most decidedly object to their being made Masons, provided they are not "free born."

Craving your pardon for thus imposing upon your valuable time, I am Sir,

Very respectfully and fraternally,

Your friend,

(Signed) CLINTON A. CILLEY

Brevet Colonel—U.S.A.

Supt. Freemens Bureau"

In checking this the following has been found:
Proceedings of Grand Lodge of New York, 1866 in the Report of Fraternal Correspondence—under North Carolina (review of 1865) on page 153, the Reviewer goes over the matter found in the N.C. Proceedings and dismisses the whole as a clumsy and wholly useless matter for them to bring up as they used no means to get in touch with the G.L. of New York to ascertain the facts in the case. Also that they had a nerve to think the G. L. of New York would "invade" the territory of N.C., etc., etc.

On page 17, 1865 of Proc. of N. C., we find E. G. Reade of Committee appointed to look into this matter with H. H. Smith and Daniel Coleman, reporting to G. L. on five pages of small type (Dec. 5, 1865), along the lines of the above letters—not particularly "against" the Negro—more against the G. L. of N. Y. Reade was elected G.M. at the above meeting and in his address on Dec. 3, 1866, page 7 in Proceedings, he devoted a single paragraph to this matter and they are still under the impression that the N. Y. Grand Lodge has something to do with it altho they seem to have asked and received a reply from N. Y. which did not satisfy them.

[XII]

LIST OF MEMBERS OF THE WILLIAMS AND WALKER COMPANY (NEGROES), WHO BECAME MEMBERS OF WAVERLY LODGE, No. 597, EDINBURGH, SCOTLAND

The following Negro brethren were made Freemasons in the above lodge, being Initiated May 2, Passed May 16 and Raised June 1, 1904. All were proposed by Brother James Halliday and seconded by Brother William Gordon. They were registered in the Books of the Grand Lodge of Scotland on May 3, 1904.

Egbert Austin Williams, 127 West 53rd St., New York, N.Y. Age 30
George William Walker, 505 Sixth Avenue, New York, N.Y. Age 31
Henry Troy, 250 Stewart Street, Montgomery, Alabama Age 28
John Edwards, 910 Sciato Street, Indianapolis, Indiana Age 26
George Catlin, 100 West 23rd St., New York, N.Y. Age 37
Peter Hampton, 329 West 35th St., New York, N.Y. Age 33
Green Henri Tapley, 3428 Dearborn Street, Chicago, Ill. Age 33

John Lubrie Hill, 505 Sixth Avenue, New York, N. Y. Age 30
James Escort Lightfoot, Hamilton, Ontario, Canada Age 33
Alexander Rogers, 18 West 134th St., New York, N.Y. Age 28

The newspapers of March 6, 1922 carried notice of the funeral of "Bert" Williams held in Masonic Temple, New York, by St. Cecile Lodge, No. 568 (white) at the request of the Grand Lodge of Scotland.

[XIII]

Anderson B. Lewis

Brother Anderson B. Lewis became the first Grand High Priest of the Grand Chapter of Royal Arch Masons of Ohio (P.H.). Prior to this he visited white lodges in Chicago and was a member of the Commandery (white) there.

The Proceedings of the Grand Lodge of Illinois are silent on these incidents but the Proceedings of the Grand Lodge of Ohio (white) for 1877 (pages 197 to 295) contain a large amount of information regarding Anderson. It appears that three lodges in Chicago, Oriental No. 33, Apollo, No. 32 and Lafayette, No. 18, were sent a note by the M. W. Grand Master regarding a protest he received from Harmony Lodge, No. 3, about a Negro, Anderson B. Lewis, visiting these lodges. All of the lodges admitted that Brother Lewis had visited them.

This same Grand Master was, at the time, first Commander of Apollo Commandery, K.T. in Chicago. At the organization meeting Lewis acted as Warder (May 20, 1845). The item says he was a well bred mulatto man, a musician. That he was of Cherokee aboriginal blood maternally and African paternally "hailing from the jurisdiction of another Grand Lodge." He was 9th on the list of the members at the chartering of the Commandery. The Grand Commandery of Illinois was formed in 1857 and Lewis is listed as a member of Apollo Commandery, No. 1, in the Proceedings of that year. The following year he is listed as "Suspended."

Research has failed to locate where Lewis was made a Mason but as he became the first Grand High Priest of the State of Ohio, it is probable that this state is that of his Masonic jurisdiction.

APPENDIX

[XIV]

JOSHUA WOODLIN

The Rev. Joshua Woodlin, was a member of Union (Unity) Lodge, No. 2 of Burlington, N. J. He was also a member of Richmond Chapter, R. A M. in the same place.

On July 12, 1848, at Burlington, the "Union Grand Lodge of A. Y. M." of New Jersey was founded. Woodlin was made Grand Secretary. He stated that he was Grand Master from 1853 to 1856, and it appears from a Proceeding of this body that he became Grand Secretary as he went out of office as Grand Master in 1856. The Proceedings of the "National Compact" Grand Lodge of the U. S., list him as "M.'.W.'.Bro. Joshua Woodlin, G.S., 1863-4, 1864-5" of New Jersey which seems to confirm that he was a Past Grand Master and still Grand Secretary as late as 1865.

In the 9th Triennial Proceedings of the "Compact" Grand Lodge he is listed as "National Grand Chaplain" on May 15, 1874.

[XV]

"FREEBORN" vs. "FREE"

One of the qualifications of a petitioner for the degrees of Freemasonry in the United States is that he shall be "freeborn."

Now, seventy-five years since any one has been born a slave in this country, this qualification falls into the category of another qualification, that a petitioner shall not be a eunuch.

Nevertheless, while the question is more academic than real, more than anything else the matter is brought into discussions on Negro Freemasonry.

We are not inclined to give this matter much attention in the present volume as the various data on it is voluminous and needful of considerable legal interpretation. We will simply call attention to one or two significant points here.

The 1723 Constitution of the Grand Lodge of England had the qualification "free-born" in it, but in 1838 the United Grand Lodge of England struck out the words and substituted the word "Free."

Dr. Joseph Robbins, Past Grand Master of the Grand Lodge of Illinois, had this to say regarding it in 1898.

"The lapse of the full period of the lifetime of a generation has substantially removed the only fundamental difficulty; and what a third of a century ago was a burning question, viz: Whether in substituting the word "free" for "free-born," fifty years ago, the Grand Lodge of England had violated a land mark, now excites only the languid interest which ever attaches to an abstraction that can never assume the concrete form."

In reality the term was without meaning in England as may be seen from a statement of Chief Justice Holt, of the Queen's Bench, England, who said:

"In England there is no such thing as a slave, and a human being never was considered a chattel to be sold for a price."

Our Grand Lodges in the United States have never seen fit to follow the Mother Grand Lodge of the world in making the change from "free-born" to "free" in their Constitutional requirements for petitioners.

On the other hand, the Negro lodges have also used the term "free-born" and they accept only such candidates. The matter, therefore, becomes entirely one of speculation and not of practice and nothing further need be discussed concerning "probabilities" or potentialities.

[XVI]

GEORGE D. STEVENS

Brother George D. Stevens, a Negro, was born in Akron, Ohio, on January 31, 1860 and died April 8, 1940 in Hartford City, Indiana. He was initiated March 25th, Passed April 29th and Raised May 13, 1925, in Blackford Lodge, No. 106, Hartford City. He received the Scottish Rite Degrees, 4–32°, November 10, 11, 12, 1925 in the Fort Wayne Scottish Rite Bodies. He was not a member of the other York Rite Bodies, however.

It was not known that Brother Stevens was a Negro until after his death. He was head of the Fort Wayne Corrugated Paper Co., had become a philanthropist and civic leader whose charities exceeded $50,000 and whose estate was five times that much. He had left his family early in life and advanced from hotel porter to one of the most influential and highly regarded manufacturers in the Fort Wayne section. Besides being a Freemason, he was an Elk and a Rotarian.

[XVII]

MINNESOTA, 1875—CORRESPONDENCE REPORT

"One of the Reportorial Corps remarked 'In the Capital of New Jersey . . . a white Lodge is making Negro Masons by wholesale.' Brother Smith says, 'This statement is correct, except in the following particulars: First—The said Lodge is not 'In the Capital of New Jersey', and Secondly—No Lodge in New Jersey makes 'Masons by wholesale.' "

[XVIII]

WILLIAM C. HANDY

The United Supreme Council, Ancient and Accepted Scottish Rite, conferred an honorary thirty-third degree upon William C. Handy, Negro composer of the song "St. Louis Blues," on May 12, 1941 in Philadelphia. Handy was among a class of fifteen candidates to receive the Masonic degree at the annual three-day conference of the Supreme Council.

BIBLIOGRAPHY

The National Masonic Union, A History of the Origin of Ancient Freemasonry Among the Colored Citizens in the United States of America, by Rev. Joshua Woodlin of Burlington, N. J., R.W. G.R. Sec. of the G. L. of N. J., and M.W.N.S.G.W. of the M.W.N.G.L. of A.Y.M. of the U.S. of N.A., Burlington, N. J. Published by the Author, 1855. Sanctioned by G.L. (George Jackson, A.G.M.,) 47 pages.

Minutes of the Proceedings of Triennial Session of the National Grand Lodge, A.Y.M. Held in Philadelphia, July 1856.
—5th Triennial held in New York, Oct. 1862.
—6th Triennial held in Baltimore, 1865.
—9th Triennial held in Louisville, 1874.

Proceedings of Grand Lodge (P.H.) of Missouri. Address of J. C. Corbin, Grand Secretary of Arkansas. Aug. 18, 1891, pages 154-159.

Massachusetts Soldiers and Sailors in the Revolutionary War. Vol. 7, page 105.

Historical Foot Prints of Modern Freemasonry Among the Colored Men in the United States and Canada, by John M. Conna.

The Negro Mason in Equity, by Samuel W. Clark, G.M. Ohio (P.H.) 1886—67 pages.

New Day—New Duty, by John D. Caldwell, G.S., G.L., of Ohio, In Proc. of 1875 of G.L. of Ohio—first 58 pages of Appendix.

Masonic Text Book, by Harrison L. Harrison

Prince Hall's Letter Book, by William H. Upton, P.G.M. (Washington) A.Q.C. Vol. XIII Part 1, 1900.

The Prince Hall Primer by Harry A. Williamson, P.D.G.M. (P.H.), N. Y. 1925.

Freemasonry in the Thirteen Colonies, by Col. J. Hugo Tatsch, 33°, 1929, 245 pages.

Coloured Freemasonry and The Pretended Dormancy of the African Grand Lodge, by Jacob Norton (Mass). Article in the Freemason's Chronicle, London, England, 1876, pages 130, 182, 196, 226, 257, 307 and 386.

The Cathedral, by Harry E. Davis, 33° (P.H.) 1938, 8 pages.

Extracts Relating to Negro Freemasonry in America, by Harry E. Davis, 33°, (P.H.) In the Journal of Negro History, October, 1936, page 411.

Negro Masonry, being a Critical Examination of objections to the legitimacy of the Masonry existing among the Negroes of America, by William H. Upton, P.G.M. (Washington) 1902, 264 pages.

An Official History of the Most Worshipful Grand Lodge Free and Accepted Masons for the State of Ohio (P.H.) by William H. Parham, P.G.M. 1906, 340 pages.

An Appeal to the Free Masons Working under the Jurisdiction of the "National Grand Lodge," by A.W.A. DeLeon, 1873, 12 pages.

National Fraternal Review, Chicago, Ill. Sept. 1931, page 4—article by Harry A. Williamson "About Alpha Lodge, No. 116."

Transactions, G.L. Ohio (P.H.) 1877 (Ohio Recognition page 21)

Address of the Grand Master and Report of a Special Committee to whom was referred the Action of the Grand Lodge of Washington on the subject of Recognizing "Negro Masonry." Published by order of the Grand Lodge of Kentucky, 1898. 32 pages.

Masonry Among Colored Men in Massachusetts—letter to Right Worshipful J. G. Findel, Honorary Grand Master of the Prince Hall Grand Lodge and General Representative thereof to the Lodges upon the Continent of Europe, by Lewis Hayden, G.M. (P.H.) 1871, 51 pages.

The Origin of the Union Grand Lodge, A.Y.M. for the State of New Jersey. Camden, 1871, 14 pages.

Proceedings of M.W. United Grand Lodge, F.A.M. for the State of New Jersey and Masonic Jurisdiction Thereunto Belonging. 1875 and 1876, 32 pages.
—Proceedings up to 1879, inclusive, 1880, 112 pages.

Negroes and Freemasonry by Harry A. Williamson, D.G.M. (P.H.) N.Y. 1920, 24 pages.

Brief Masonry History by J. C. Parker, Detroit, Mich. 1929, 47 pages.

Court of Heroines of Jericho by Moses Dickson, 1895, 72 pages.

A Masonic Vade Mecum by B. F. Adams, Grand Lecturer for Mo. (P.H.) n.d., 92 pages.

Constitution and General Regulations for the Government of Courts of the Adoptive Rite or Female Freemasonry. Philadelphia, Pa. 1872, 8 pages.

A Charge Delivered to the African Lodge, June 23, 1797 at Menotomy, Mass., by the Right Worshipful Prince Hall, published by the Desire of the Members of Said Lodge, 1797 (obtained through the courtesy of Bro. August C. Fleet from H. E. Pickersgill and printed by Arthur A. Schomburg, Grand Secretary, G.L. of N. Y. (P.H.)

Joint Bulletin of the Supreme Councils, A. & A.S.R. (Prince Hall Affiliation) 1908, 38 pages.

Official History of Freemasonry Among the Colored People of North America, by William H. Grimshaw, P.D.G.M. of D.C. (P.H.) 1903, 393 pages.

Prince Hall and His Followers, by George W. Crawford, 33°, 1914, 96 pages.

Bibliography of Negro Freemasonry. MS compiled by Harry A. Williamson, P.G.H. of the G.L. of N. Y. (P.H.)

Prince Hall Masonry in New York State, by Harry A. Williamson, P.G.H. of the G.L. of N. Y. (P. H.) in the "New York Age" (newspaper) serially in 1936.

A Chronological History of Prince Hall Masonry 1784-1932, by Harry A. Williamson, P.G.H. of the G.L. of N. Y. (P.H.) in the "New York Age" (newspaper) serially 1934 starting April 7.

Proceedings of various Negro and Caucasian Grand Lodges and other Masonic bodies, too numerous to list.

Minute books of various Grand and subordinate bodies of Negro Freemasonry.

Grand Lodge records in various jurisdictions.

INDEX

A

Abbott, Leon S., 62
African Lodge, No. 370, 34
African Lodge, No. 459, charter, 20
  degrees conferred, 29
  first meeting, 22
  not constituted or officers
    installed, 23
  Not part of Grand Lodge of Mass.
    (white), 25
  Removed from English
    Register, 35
  Renumbered 370, 34
Allen, Bishop Richard, 34
Alpha Lodge, No. 116,
  first officers, 84
  chartered, 83
  charter arrested, 90
  charter restored, 93
  membership statistics, 104
American Lodge of Research,
  F. & A. M., N. Y., 22
Ancient & Accepted Scottish Rite
  (Negro), 57
  Louisiana Group, 62
Anderson, William J., 108
Army Lodge, No. 441—
  Masons made in, 11

B

Baker, Phoebe—
  Second wife of Prince Hall, 8
Baldwin, Israel, 82, 83, 84, 86
Bierce, Lucius V.,
  P.G.M. of Ohio, 12
Bondman, Richard, 7
Bulow, de, Baron A. Hugo, 59

C

Caldwell, John D., G.S. of Ohio, 12
Canadian Colored Lodge, 108
Cannon, Henry R.,
  G.M. of New Jersey, 78
Cannon, James
  of New Jersey, 51

Carson, Enoch T., P.M. of Ohio, 12
Cerneau, Joseph, 63
Chillicothe Warrant, The, 111
Chivalric Masonry (Negro), 55
Clark, Daniel W., 104
Clark, Samuel W., 11, 73
Clinton Lodge, No. 54,
  Savannah, Ga., 50
Constitution of the U. S. A.—
  Amendments, 81
Crawford, George W., XI
Cruse, Howard R.,
  G.M. of New Jersey, 103
Cryptic Masonry (Negro), 54
Cumberland, Duke of, 19
Cushite Lodge—Petition for, 79
Cynthia Lodge, No. 155,
  Cincinnati, Ohio, 85

D

Daughters of Isis, 71
Davis, Harry E., XI
Davis, Jonathan, 70
De Grasse, John V.,
  P.G.M. of Mass. (P.H.), 14
Delaney, Martin R., M.D., X
Dias, John W., 105
Dickson, Moses, 69
District of Columbia,
  Negro Grand Lodge, 75
Drayton, Paul, 50

E

Edwards, George B.,
  Grand Marshal of N. J., 89, 90
Ethiopian Supreme Council
  for the U. S. A., 51

F

First New Jersey Negroes Vote, 81
First Nine Members of Alpha Lodge,
  No. 116, Case History, 84

129